DREAM BIG!

How to REACH
for Your STARS!

DREAM BIG!

How to REACH for Your STARS!

ABIGAIL HARRISON

PHILOMEL BOOKS

PHILOMEL BOOKS

An imprint of Penguin Random House LLC, New York

First published in the United States of America by Philomel,
an imprint of Penguin Random House LLC, 2021

Text copyright © 2021 by Abigail Harrison

Illustrations copyright © 2021 by Sarah J. Coleman

Philomel Books is a registered trademark of Penguin Random House LLC.

Visit us online at penguinrandomhouse.com.

Library of Congress Control Number: 2020948510

Printed in the United States of America

ISBN 9780593116753

10 9 8 7 6 5 4 3 2 1

Edited by Talia Benamy.
Design by Monique Sterling.
Text set in Archer.

Dedicated to all the big dreamers out there who will make the Mars generation a reality. Chasing after your dreams will make the future a better place—both on Earth and off it!

And to all those supporting big dreamers (moms, dads, caretakers, teachers, mentors—you know who you are!), who help guide dreamers toward reaching for their stars.

And finally, to my own mom, for showing me through her constant love and support that dreams are worth chasing after. Love you to Mars and back, Mom!

Contents

Introduction

Decide in your heart of hearts what really excites and challenges you and start moving your life in that direction.

—Commander Chris Hadfield, astronaut

Let me start out by making one thing super clear: I believe in you and your awesomeness. Really, I do! I know it's true because I know you have a dream—maybe readily apparent or perhaps buried deep down—and I also know that you have the ability to achieve it given the right skills and tools. And I know it's true even more so because you're reading this book, which will help you find your dreams and learn everything you need to know to chase them!

I know from personal experience that it's never too early to find your life's passion and start chasing after your dreams—and, as you do so, to make a huge impact on the world. I discovered my dream when I was only about four or five years old, which was when I decided that I wanted to become an astronaut and the first astronaut to walk on Mars. I spent most of my childhood hearing that my dreams weren't realistic, that I would someday grow out of them and I should instead choose something more attainable (i.e., more "mainstream"). But I never grew out of my big dream—rather than changing or fading over time, my dreams only became more vivid and tangible. As I got older I decided that I couldn't wait for a "right time" to start chasing my dreams—I had to just get started. In the face of everything in the world telling me that my dream was unrealistic, I chose to take matters into my own hands and define for myself what I was capable of.

I haven't fully achieved my dream yet (sadly twenty-two is a bit young to be sent to space), but I have spent over a decade chasing after my out-of-this-world dream and have accomplished some incredible things during that time. I've worked in a NASA astrobiology lab as a scientist; conducted research in Siberia, one of the most remote corners of the world; and reached the most incredible highs and lows on this planet by receiving advanced scuba-dive training, going skydiving, and earning a pilot's license. I've met countless astronauts and other space industry professionals, toured spacecraft development and launch facilities around the entire world, been invited to speak at hundreds of locations (including in front of Congress!), worked in collaboration with an astronaut during his time on the International Space Station, and become a social media influencer with almost a million followers. On top of that, at the age of eighteen, I co-founded a successful nonprofit to support the next generation in achieving great things. I never expected to have any of these experiences, and I definitely never imagined that at just twenty-two years old I would be considered an expert on the future of human space exploration, a world-renowned advocate for my generation, an author, or the founder of a successful and impactful nonprofit organization.

But for all that I could never have predicted what my future would hold, I also know that these things didn't just happen to me—they were a direct result of my knowing what my dreams were and chasing after them with unabashed abandon. Now I want to share how I went about aspiring to achieve the impossible, breaking barriers, and changing the world for the better— and how you can too! In this book I'll share with you everything I've learned throughout my journey about how to discover and achieve big dreams.

Before we really dive in, let me give you a hint: chasing your dreams involves just a few broad steps. Once you have those under your belt, you'll be well on your way. Those steps are:

☑ Know clearly what your dream is.

☑ Do your research about it!

☑ Form a plan of how *you* can achieve it.

☑ Be willing to be vocal and stand up for your dream.

Of course, there are specific strategies to each of these ideas, and we'll talk about them over the course of this book. But if I've learned one thing through my experiences, it is that having and reaching for a dream can be incredibly powerful. Finding your dreams and having the knowledge and skills to act on them gives you the ability to garner support from those around you, plan for your future, and cultivate bravery in the face of uncertainty. *You* can change the world, and you don't have to wait to start doing it.

This book will expose you to the lessons I've learned about finding and achieving dreams and guide you through a series of interactive, self-reflective activities designed to help you find your dreams, grow your confidence, and learn the skills necessary to chase after success. Join me as I show you step by step how I pursued my goals and dreams and how you can too. Let's get going and start dreaming big!

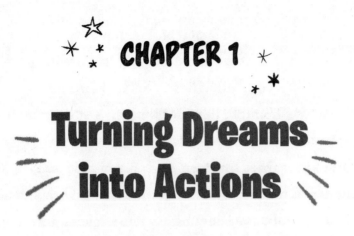

CHAPTER 1

Turning Dreams into Actions

Nothing is impossible. The word itself says "I'm possible!"

—Audrey Hepburn, actress and humanitarian

One of my earliest memories is of looking up at the night sky and dreaming about the stars. I must have been about four or five years old, and I remember wondering how many of them there were. I wondered what else was out there. But most of all I wondered whether I might someday travel among them.

I've known for as long as I can remember that I wanted to become an astronaut. That was my dream: to head toward the stars, walk in space, and see those glowing balls of gas and plasma unfiltered by our planet's atmosphere. And while that dream never changed, as I got older, it became more sophisticated, more nuanced, and more concrete. I began to think more critically about how I could go about making this dream of walking in space a reality. I knew that it wouldn't just happen on its own, that no one was going to hand it to me on a silver platter. And so I dug in.

As I did, I learned that turning a dream into reality is, above all, a matter of making a plan, setting goals, and taking action toward those goals. I've spent nearly two decades now developing and chasing my own astronomical dream, and a decade sharing that dream with the entire world. During that time I've met people who have *achieved* all kinds of massive dreams; those people include actors, lawyers, newscasters, politicians, researchers, and, of course, my personal favorite, astronauts. I've also met countless people, of all ages, who are working toward their dreams. I've spoken at conferences and in classrooms about goal setting and dream chasing, received letters and correspondences from people searching for their purpose, and interacted on social media with people at every stage of the dreaming process. What I've learned from my own journey, as well as from all of these other journeys that I have crossed paths with, is that the road toward accomplishing a goal is rarely straightforward or smooth. But even as we acknowledge that, we can also find ways to make our paths simpler to follow and our dreams easier to achieve.

What do those ways look like? you might be wondering. Well, there are a few steps, but the very first thing to do is to figure out what it is you're truly passionate about—this is key, because only once you've pinpointed your passions can you start to shape them into a dream. Then you can determine how to make those passions more defined, how to craft them into a specific goal. Once you've defined your dream in that way, it's time to step back, to truly evaluate it, and to decide whether it's ultimately feasible. At that point, you can go about making your big dream a reality.

Welcome to *Dream Big!*, your personal guide to all things dreaming and goal setting. In this first chapter we're going to dive right into what a dream is, how you can find yours, and what the path toward achieving it might look like.

WHAT IS A DREAM?

Dreams matter. Truly, the importance of dreams is something that I'd put on the same level of importance as the fundamental truth that gravity holds us to Earth. That's a big statement, I know—so let me explain what I mean, starting by defining just what a dream is.

Of course, in the most literal sense, a dream can refer to what plays through our minds when we sleep, or when we allow our thoughts to wander while awake. When that happens, it means we've handed control of our thoughts over to our subconscious, and our complex brains create imaginary scenes. These types of dreams can be good (one of my personal favorites is eating ice cream in bed while watching my favorite TV show), bad (like the nightmare I know we've all had of showing up late to class, taking a test in a language you don't understand, and then realizing you're not wearing any pants), or somewhere in between (like the one I had of riding a giraffe through a city of clouds while harmonizing show ballads).

In this book, though, we'll talk about dreams a bit differently. Here, a dream is a cherished goal, a dearly held ambition, an aspiration for our future that we strive toward and hope for. And much like the force of gravity to which I've just compared the weight dreams can carry, dreams are an unchangeable, constant force. Unlike gravity, however, dreams don't follow any sort of law of physics; instead, they are part of what I like to think of as the laws of humanity. Having dreams is what makes us human. Dreaming allows us to look past ourselves, to look past our current situation and reality, and to see what can be. Dreams are human creativity and hope taking shape.

When thinking about dreams, I often separate them into two categories: general and personal. People can have both general and personal dreams, but the ways in which they engage with those two types of dreams might vary. Let me explain.

General dreams are those with outcomes that we might hope for, but that we do not hope to personally accomplish. For example, some general dreams might include the dream of peace on Earth or faster-than-light travel, or even the dream that the

Vikings might someday win the Super Bowl. Personal dreams are, as you might have guessed from the name, dreams that include a more personal connection, apply to us as individuals in some way, and are tangibly achievable through our own actions. These types of dreams might include becoming a leader at the United Nations and working to minimize conflict around the world; becoming an astrophysicist to research the speed of light and develop faster-than-light travel; or becoming a football player, joining the Vikings, and leading the team to Super Bowl glory. Despite how different all of these personal dreams are, the unifying factor in each of them is that they are focused on future events that the dreamer might someday achieve through the right combination of hard work, natural talent, and luck.

It's important to keep the distinction between general and personal dreams in mind as you move along your dreaming path. Forgetting this can pose a danger, because general and personal dreams can sometimes be *very* closely related to one another—or at least seem that way, especially when a personal dream stems from a general dream. It can also be easy to think of the two of them as being connected, because that can help make your own personal dream become more concrete in your mind.

But without going from the general to the personal, you'll find yourself facing a roadblock on the path toward achieving your dream, because the general dream might just seem too large. However, starting with the general dream can help you narrow down your vision of what you want your personal dream to be. Once you've done that, you can start to make plans and take actions in your life to accomplish your personal dream.

I'll give you an example of what I mean. Let's say that, like me, you hope that someday humans will walk on Mars—that's a general dream. But if you take that hope for the future and start to imagine, also like me, that someday *you, personally,* will set foot on the Red Planet—that begins to make it a personal dream. One broad general dream can allow for any number of specific personal dreams: hoping generally that humans will walk on Mars might also lead you to imagine that you will one day be a flight surgeon, or an electrical engineer, or any of the other hundreds of specialties that are involved in the space program and that will make human travel to Mars a real possibility in the future.

Identifying Your Personal Dream!

Distinguishing between general and personal dreams can be difficult! This activity will help you understand and recognize the differences—so that you can determine what your own personal dream is. Use the table on the next page to get thinking about some general dreams you might have, and to then figure out the personal connection you have to them.

GENERAL DREAMS	PERSONAL DREAMS
Have humans walk on Mars.	Become a mechanical engineer for the space program to help build the rockets to send humans to Mars.

As we discuss dreams in this book, we'll be looking at personal dreams and talking about how to work to achieve them. But before we can do any of that, we need to take a step back and figure out one very important thing: how to discover, identify, and formulate *your* dreams.

FINDING *YOUR* DREAM(S)

I'm lucky enough to have known what my passion is, and to some extent what my dream is, my entire life. If, when I was born, I could have spoken, I probably would have been shouting, "Space. Send me to spaaaace!" But since I wasn't a miracle baby, I had to wait a few more years before I could vocalize what it was that I intended to do with my future. Of course, it's also possible that I acquired the desire for space travel at some point after birth, but before my brain was very good at forming and storing long-term memories. Either way, I don't remember a point at which I came upon my passion for space and my dream to become an astronaut. It was merely something I grew up knowing I aspired to, something that, every time I thought about it, filled me with excitement. When I was too young to read, I would stare up at the night sky and dream of someday flying among the stars, and once I was old enough to read, I remember voraciously consuming all the space books I could get my hands on.

Space, and Mars in particular, was an all-consuming passion for me. Wanting to become an astronaut was a part of my identity. When I was sitting in my first-grade classroom and the teacher asked us to say one thing about ourselves as an introduction, mine was, "My name is Abby and I want to become an astronaut!" As sure as I could proclaim my name, raise enough fingers to show how old I was, or rattle off my home address, I could say what my future goals were. Likewise, when I went to college later on, I introduced myself to people there by handing over a business card listing my website, AstronautAbby.com.

But while my desire to become an astronaut has been tied to my identity for as long as I can remember, I know that for most people, this isn't usually the case. In fact, most people have to do a bit (or maybe a lot!) of digging before they can unearth their dreams.

And here's the scoop about starting that digging: since a dream is a future goal that you aspire to achieve because it pertains to something you are passionate about, the first step in finding your dream (or dreams) is to discover what your passions are. And trust me, that alone is no small task!

PASSION: WHAT'S THAT?

Passion is a strong feeling for something that you care about, a feeling that goes beyond a simple interest, that indicates the next level up. I like to think of the distinction between a regular, run-of-the-mill hobby and a more definite passion as a sort of equation: a passion is an interest you have + an extreme focus on that interest + activities related to that interest that you love to do + a deeper meaning that you ascribe to that interest.

It won't come as a surprise to you to hear that my passion is space. Space is something that I find really interesting, nearly to a level of obsession. I (almost) never get tired of reading about, talking about, or even just thinking about space. The deeper meaning that I ascribe to this interest—and what I believe helps turn it from just an interest into a true passion—is that I believe that space exploration holds the keys to our universe and will be integral to the future of humanity.

Just for the record: you can have more than one passion, and your passions can come in different levels of seriousness! I am very serious about my passion for space—serious enough that I want to dedicate my entire life to it, and am willing to risk everything to explore it. But I also have *other* passions. I have a passion for dancing ballet, a passion for playing fiddle, a passion for designing my own clothes, and many more. Each of these are activities that I am highly interested in, love to do, and find some deeper meaning in.

One quick—but important—note here: having a passion for something doesn't mean that acting on it won't be difficult. It doesn't mean that you won't have to work for it. There's a saying that goes, "Choose a job you love, and you will never have to

work a day in your life," and let me tell you, I can't stand that saying. It's just plain not true. Loving your work, or being passionate about what you do, does not mean that you won't have to put any effort into it, that you'll enjoy every single moment of it, or that your journey will be easy and straightforward all the time. But having a passion means that you love something enough—and find enough meaning in it—to invest your time and energy to pursue it and, especially, to persevere if the going gets tough. With that said, we get to the obvious question: How do you figure out what your passion is, what makes all the hard work worth it?

FINDING *YOUR* PASSION(S)

Finding your passion may seem like a daunting task, but I promise it doesn't have to be difficult! The first step is simply to ask yourself, *What is it that I want?* This might seem like a rather obvious place to start, but let me break it down a bit further.

First off, remember that when you're asking yourself this question, you probably don't want to answer it by thinking about what you want *right this instant.* That is undoubtedly a useful question, and it's one that might even be able to help direct you toward your passion. But it could (and likely will) also elicit answers such as, "Huh, I'd really like some ice cream," or "Man, right now I want to go play basketball." Neither of those answers is bad, of course, but they likely won't lead you to figure out a long-term passion for yourself. If you answered that you'd like some ice cream, it's certainly possible that you truly are passionate about ice cream. Perhaps you dream of inventing a new flavor or of running an ice cream shop. Similarly, if you answered that you'd like to play basketball, you could really have a passion

for basketball. Your future might lie in the NBA or in designing sportswear specific to basketball. But it's more likely that you answered that you want ice cream because you were hungry at the time of the question and perhaps saw someone eating ice cream earlier in the day, or that you answered that you want to play basketball because you heard a basketball being dribbled outside or glanced at the basketball jersey hanging in your room. Ultimately, while the question of *What is it that I want right now?* is not to be discounted, it usually isn't the definitive be-all and end-all for defining a dream.

To properly consider the question of what we want, in order to really figure out what our passions are, it's important to consider not only what we want in the moment but also what we want for the future. I recommend that you not only ask yourself *What is it that I want?* but that you also ask a series of questions with future times attached, such as:

* ★ *What is it that I want tomorrow?*
* ★ *What is it that I want for one week from now? One month from now? One year from now?*
* ★ *What is it that I want in five, ten, or even twenty years from now?*

Asking yourself these types of questions can help you focus in on what's really important to you—what you're passionate about—and provide some context for why you want these things, and they can help lead you to thinking about what your actual dreams could be. Thinking objectively about what it is we want for ourselves at different points in the future can help us to be more focused and accurate in homing in on a passion and a dream.

Try to answer these questions as truthfully as you can, without pressuring or judging yourself. Don't worry at this point about whether your passions and dreams seem realistic or completely out there. Our world is constantly changing, and something that might seem completely fanciful right now could become a real thing in the near future. Likewise, don't concern yourself too much with the size or magnitude of your passions and dreams right now. It's A-okay if your passion is for volley-ball and your dream is to make it onto your school's team next year. It's also A-okay if your passion leads you to a dream that is as seemingly out of this world as mine might sound. A dream that challenges you in any way is a great dream to have, so if your passions lead you toward a dream that feels monumental or even scares you a little bit to think about, don't worry—that actually means you're on the right path!

Let's pause here for a moment, because I know this isn't as easy as snapping your fingers and coming up with answers to the questions I'm posing. So let's say that you've gone ahead and asked yourself what it is that you want—now or for the future—and you find that you're just not sure. You're not sure what you want now, or in twenty years, or anywhere in between. Don't worry! We're not done with the "finding your passion" strategies yet! Here are a few more questions you can ask yourself that might help you figure out what it is that you're passionate about:

1. **Why do I do the things I do right now?** To help give yourself some context, write out a list of the things you've done today, or in the past week, or over the last weekend.

Take a close look at your list and ask yourself, *Why did I do each of these things?* Are there any points on the list that you did because you just wanted to?

2. **What scares me?** Think about your answer to this question, and then think about why it scares you. Is there something that comes to mind that makes you just shudder and think, "I could never do that!" If so, ask yourself why that thing scares you so much—and then ask yourself whether maybe, just maybe, you might be able to do the thing after all. (I'll let you in on a little secret: even though I knew I wanted to be an astronaut, which would mean flying as high as humanly possible, I was scared of heights for a long time when I was growing up!)

3. **What makes me happy?** Make a list of your hobbies, and then next to each one write out what it is about that activity that makes you happy, what makes you want to keep doing it. Maybe even rate them on a scale of one to ten based on which ones you like the most.

4. **Who do I admire?** Make a list of people you admire and then think about why you admire them. Would you want to do what they do?

5. **What do I want to do when I grow up?** Make a list of ten

dream jobs. Once you've done that, look at them as a group and consider: Are there any similarities among them?

I hope those questions helped spark something in your mind as you work on figuring out what it is that you're passionate about. But even if none of those questions evoked a strong feeling in you (which is to say, even if you still haven't found your "thing" yet), do not fear! Self-evaluation and self-assessment are not the only paths forward when discovering a passion. It's entirely possible that you haven't encountered your passion yet, which would make it impossible for you to know what it is or how to describe it. The only way to find your passion, if you haven't yet encountered it, is to try new things. Lots of them. Seriously . . . LOTS!

Branching out gives you your best chance to come across something you're passionate about, because to find your passion, you have to be engaged with the world around you. But no doubt about it, trying new things can be really hard! In order to try something new (or many somethings new!) you have to be ready to seek out opportunities, be open to new experiences, and be prepared to be bad at something. That's a really hard thing—to be bad at something. And it's even harder to try many things and possibly be bad at them! But the only way to find things that you're passionate about—to find your dreams—is to try new things, especially things that are different from what you're familiar with or have done before. If you want to find your passions and define your dreams, you have to create a shift within your mind so that you no longer fear failure. You have to give yourself the permission and the freedom to be bad at things without judging yourself too harshly or basing your self-worth on your achievement rate. And when you finally do hit on the right fit for you, even if you're bad to begin with, chances are you'll get better with time!

If you're still not sure what it is that you want to do or what your dream is, just be patient! I know that can be difficult advice to follow, but truly, the way to find your passion, and subsequently define your dream, is to try new things and continuously evaluate your experiences. Try lots of new things and ask yourself questions like, *Do I enjoy this? Why or why not?* or, *Could I see myself doing this in the future, whether in one or five or even ten years?* or, *Does this thing or activity hold a deeper meaning or connection for me, something that makes it more personally worthwhile than the other things I enjoy?* If you keep doing that, eventually you *will* find something that you are passionate about. Sometimes it just takes time. Be patient and kind with yourself, and sooner or later, you'll have no problem finding your passions and your dreams.

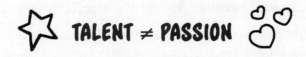

☆ TALENT ≠ PASSION ♡♡

I know I've already talked about the idea of being bad at something when you first start. I want to come back to that point for a moment, though, because it's important to prepare yourself and give yourself permission to be bad at something for a *while*. Maybe even *forever*. Because the truth of the matter is that passion is not the same thing as talent, and talent is not the same thing as passion. Passion ≠ talent. I bring up this notion again because it is *so* incredibly important to understand the difference and not equate the two.

Talent is something that you are born with. Talent isn't something that you get to choose, nor is it something that you can achieve through hard work. A talent might be a great singing voice, or the ability to remember long lists of numbers without practicing, or being able to jump higher, run faster, and go for longer than others. A talent exists before you even try something and shows up before you practice much at all.

But just because you're good at something doesn't mean you'll love it, or even like it. And being talented at something doesn't necessarily make it your passion. It can be easy to mistake talent for passion because we, as humans, like to achieve things, and so we'll often do what we're good at, even if we're not truly enjoying ourselves. On the flip side, yet equally important: being bad at something (or even just so-so at it) doesn't mean that it's not your passion. Having a particular talent should not define what your passion is or what your dreams can be.

FORMING A DREAM OUT OF YOUR PASSION (FINALLY!)

Now that you've spent some time coming up with your passions, you can (finally!) start to make use of those passions and search for your dreams. Just like there was an equation for what makes up a passion (a hearty dose of interest, a strong splash of enjoyment, and a hefty sprinkle of deeper meaning and connection), dreams also have an equation, and it's a bit simpler than the one for passions—there are only two components! In short, dreams are: your passion + a goal. The good news here is that you've already done the hard work, which is discovering what you're passionate about. Now all you have to do is search within that passion for something that you hope to accomplish! For me, it was transitioning my passion for space into a desire to go to space, and then coming up with the more specific dream of being the first astronaut to walk on Mars. Not all dreams that you form have to be lifelong aspirations like this—but they can be. The beautiful thing about a dream is that, as long as it's fueled by a passion, the rest of the details (the magnitude of the dream, the time it'll take to accomplish, and so on) don't really matter.

Your dream might be as large in magnitude as a lifelong career, or as small as a single action. It might be about attaining something that's forty years down the road, or it could entail reaching for something that's just a couple weeks, or even days, away. Dreams aren't defined by the time it takes to reach them, or the relative effort. Dreams are defined by what fuels you to chase after them—a dream is something you go after because you are passionate about it.

Express Your Dreams!

WHAT DO YOU DREAM ABOUT?	WHAT ARE YOU PASSIONATE ABOUT?
Which of these passions and dreams line up?	

⚡ FINDING FEASIBILITY IN YOUR BIG DREAM ⚡

As you're going through the process of shaping your passion into a dream, one thing to consider is the feasibility of the goal you've set for yourself as part of your new dream. I don't at all say this to scare you off from chasing big dreams or to tamp down your excitement in any way. In fact, I raise it because being honest with yourself will make your dreams stronger, will help you home in on a dream that's authentic to you, and will help you handle anyone who doesn't believe in your dream.

The truth of the matter is that you can't really defend something unless you've considered it from all angles—and that goes for your dreams as well. It's absolutely vital to ask the hard questions about any dream that you are forming or chasing—questions like, "What are my odds?" or, "What will I lose or gain

by striving toward this, and am I willing to take that risk?" Addressing these questions improves your ability to pursue your dreams and makes it harder for the haters to hate as you go.

While engaging in this kind of personal assessment, you might find that your passion—or maybe just one of your passions—is something you're just really not very good at, not at the beginning, not after a couple months, or maybe not even after years of practice. And this is *okay*. At the end of the day, some of your passions can remain passions without becoming dreams. In my life, music definitely fits into the category of "passion but not dream." As much as I love music—and even tried my hand at learning to play the violin—it's just not something I'm especially good at (and that's putting it lightly). So while I know that I can wholeheartedly appreciate music in the course of my daily life, I also recognize that I don't have to attach any concrete goal to it and make it into a full-fledged dream.

All of which is to say: it is important to try new things in order to discover what you are passionate about, but it is equally important to understand not only that talent and passion are different, but also that not all of your passions need to become dreams. An important part of a dream is that it's realistic, that there is some semblance of possibility in it. That through the right combination of hard work, talent, and good luck, it can be achievable. Creating a dream is all about being honest with yourself while pushing your boundaries.

TAKING ACTION: BIG DREAMS GROW FROM A SERIES OF SMALL ACTIONS

Thinking about accomplishing a dream can be daunting—often the goal you're trying to reach will feel impossibly far away. It might seem difficult to start taking actions toward your big dream because it seems like, in order to reach a big dream, you'd need to start with a big action. But the truth of it is that big dreams don't require big actions; they just require a consistent pattern of small actions. Every successful person, every person out there who has accomplished their dream, did so through a long series of small actions—which is lucky, because it's much easier to start down a path when all it takes is one small step. As we saw with the moon landings, a single small action is often the catalyst for an incredible future.

The first small step that each and every dreamer needs to take if they hope to be successful is to make a plan. To create your plan, start by marking down what your dream is, where you stand right now along the path toward achieving it, and when you hope to ultimately accomplish it. Next, make a list of all the things you will need to do, large or small, in order to make your dream a reality. Add in approximate dates by which to accomplish each item on the list, and then begin to create detailed steps to reach each of these milestones.

I made my first plan for becoming an astronaut when I was eleven years old. I had just had a conversation with my mom in which she asked me questions similar to those we've just discussed about how feasible my dream actually was, given that out of 7 billion people on the planet, fewer than six hundred had ever been to outer space. After laying it all out for me and hearing that I was still going full steam ahead for my dream (and maybe even more so than before I had learned just how difficult it would be—I've always loved a good challenge), my mom challenged me to create my first written plan of how I would go about accomplishing my dream.

It was this plan that led me to go to Space Camp when I was thirteen, that influenced me to study Mandarin Chinese when I was fourteen (and later Russian as well), that led me to becoming an advanced scuba diver, that guided my choices of where to go to college and what to major in, that allowed me to work in a NASA astrobiology research laboratory at nineteen, that inspired me to become a pilot at twenty-one, and so much more.

I didn't follow the plan that I wrote out at age eleven to the letter—in fact, there are very few specific parts of it that ended up actually happening in my life. As I continued onward over the next decade, I diverged and then rejoined with my plan, as well as revised and sometimes even scrapped the plan and started a new one, all to deal with the chaotic path that real life presents. The point of making a plan isn't to create a strict set of rules to live by or to mandate that only by way of this very specific set of actions and circumstances will you achieve your dream. No, the point of making a plan is to take that first action, the first small step toward your dream. Writing out a plan can help you organize what things you think you'll need to accomplish in order to achieve your dream, and to think about when you'll need to accomplish them, and how. It breaks up what can otherwise seem like an insurmountable task into smaller steps that are easily achievable, one by one, to eventually lead to your big dream. Most importantly, writing out a plan forces you to engage in self-reflection and assessment, necessary actions to keep you focused on what your goal really is and to go down a path that will allow you to reach your dreams.

Before we move on to the rest of the book, I'd like to make one point perfectly clear, and that is: you can have more than one dream. Dreams come in different shapes and sizes, and sometimes a dream may grow or fade—you don't have to have the same dream your entire life! You might have some dreams that are specific to certain points in your life or to certain activities, while other dreams might revolve around things you aspire to accomplish unrelated to anything else you're doing. When I was in high school, I dreamed of becoming the captain of my school's gymnastics team. I also dreamed of meeting one of my favorite authors (Tamora Pierce) and of writing a book. All of these dreams existed side by side with my overarching dream of someday walking on Mars. I chose to stick with my Mars dream, to try to see it through to the end, and that choice worked for me. But everyone can and should do this differently!

Make the Impossible Possible! ✒

The first part of making the impossible possible is creating a mind-set shift. Just like Audrey Hepburn did in the quote at the beginning of the chapter, you need to split up the word "impossible" so it becomes "I'm possible!" What I've learned is that often the biggest thing holding back a dream is our own inability to see ourselves doing it. Are your wild dreams actually wild? The truth is, probably

1) OVERCOME FEAR OF **HEIGHTS**.
2) WORK HARD IN **SCHOOL**.
3) BECOME A **PILOT**.
4) LEARN **RUSSIAN** & **MANDARIN**.
5) WORK FOR **NASA**.

not. We're all our own worst critic, and when we see things from other people's perspectives it turns out that unrealistic dreams don't seem so far off. What is needed is the confidence to tackle the big dream one small piece at a time. Try the activity on this page to help yourself visualize your dreams and see them more realistically by planning out some of the small actions that will help make them a reality.

* ☺ DRAW YOURSELF

achieving _your_ dream.

WRITE OUT the BASIC STEPS to GET THERE!
1,
2,
3.

You've probably heard the name **Audrey Hepburn**—she's widely considered to be one of the greatest movie stars of all time. And that's not just an opinion—she's actually one of only fifteen people ever to have received all four major entertainment-industry awards (the Oscar, the Emmy, the Grammy, and the Tony). Throughout her life, Audrey always followed her passions and let them guide her to stardom. Growing up in Nazi-occupied Holland during the height of World War II, she fought back against the injustice she saw by performing in secret ballet recitals to raise money for the resistance effort. She made a difference in the world by following her passions and doing what she loved. Audrey became a Hollywood actress because she spent her entire life following her passions—first for ballet, then for modeling, and finally for acting! Just like Audrey, if you follow your passions in life with unending dedication, you'll undoubtedly achieve your dreams.

The single most important thing to remember as you go is that dreams are at the heart of humanity, and each and every one of us has a dream, but sometimes finding and recognizing these dreams can be difficult. Dreams are achieved by way of actionable goals that are based in passion, so to find our dreams we have to first discover what it is that we're passionate about. And now that we're well on our way, I hope you'll join me as we dive into figuring out just how to make our dreams a reality!

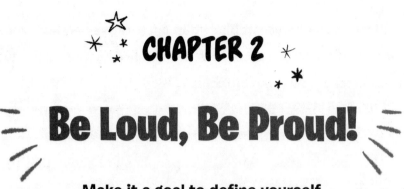

CHAPTER 2

Be Loud, Be Proud!

Make it a goal to define yourself.
Find the strength to tell your story.

—Glory Edim, writer and entrepreneur

From the moment I decided I wanted to become an astronaut, I've talked about it incessantly. I'd tell family, friends, teachers—anyone who would listen—about my dreams of going to space and walking on Mars. It was something I was excited about, and I wanted to let people know that. The people around me who heard my story became my greatest and most fundamental supporters—they became a community that provided resources and opportunities to reach my goals, and empowered me to believe unendingly in myself.

Big dreams are not accomplished in a vacuum—unless, like me, your big dream is to be an astronaut, then yes, that would be *quite literally* accomplished in the vacuum of space. But even my dream won't be accomplished in a figurative vacuum. What I mean by this is that success is not reached by one individual alone. Instead, achieving big dreams is only possible through the collective actions of a conglomerate of people—a community—that supports one another in achieving their dreams.

It's easy to look at successful people and believe that they accomplished their dreams all on their own. We see an image of them that is filtered through the lens of news outlets or social media, both of which are highly curated to show a certain story—but that story may not necessarily be the whole truth. It's much easier to showcase a single person at the pinnacle of their success than it is to incorporate everyone who contributed to that success.

On top of that, what we see of success is almost exclusively the end product. We don't often have a record of successful people during their early stages—the time before they're successful—because, logically, fewer people would have been paying attention to them then. But because of that, we miss out on seeing how their dreams brewed and when they started to take the first steps toward their future, as well as the struggles they had to overcome and the doubts they experienced along the way. And for each of those points missed, we also miss seeing all the other people who played a role on that more visible person's road to success. But even if we don't see those people, we know they must have been there, because the truth is, as much as everything in the media or elsewhere seems to tell us otherwise, *it's nearly impossible to achieve great things all alone.* The support of a community, whatever that community may look like, is essential to success.

Some people are lucky enough to have a community or support system already built in. But for anyone who doesn't, the obvious question to ask is: How do you go about finding your community? Well, the answer is to be loud and be proud! And even if you have a community ready to go, it's still great to be loud and proud! It's important to speak up and share your dreams, no matter how outlandish they may seem. We all need a supportive community around us, and speaking up is the first step toward finding and cultivating it. And while those might not be habits that come naturally to everyone, both being audaciously proud of your dream and speaking out fearlessly about it are skills that can be learned and practiced.

Each of us belong to many communities. Some of those might include the school or summer camp you go to, the neighborhood you live in or hometown you're from, the sports team you play on, the church/synagogue/mosque/temple you attend, and the family and friends you spend time with. Finding the communities that will support our dreams is not always easy, but it's definitely worth the effort. Being loud and proud about your dreams can help you figure out who your cheerleaders are and where to focus your attention to find the support that will help you accomplish your dreams.

Accomplishing my dream of becoming an astronaut is a great example of how it takes a community to fulfill a dream. Astronauts are the most visbile part of space exploration

(although the *Curiosity* rover gave them a run for their money in the popularity contest!), so they're often what we think of when we think of space travel. But the real truth is that it takes tens of thousands of people to send a single astronaut to space, including the communities that support them while they're striving toward this dream, the people who train them to go to space, the scientists and engineers who design and build the capsules and rockets that will send them to space, and the entire crew at ground control during each mission. Much like how each space mission, and each astronaut in space, is the result of tens of thousands of people working together, your dreams will also be the result not only of your hard work but also of all the people who support you on your way to your dream. Learning to be loud and proud allows them to join you on your journey!

WHAT DOES IT ACTUALLY MEAN TO BE LOUD AND PROUD?

First, let me start with the obvious: being loud has nothing to do with volume and everything to do with effect. Being loud is all about sharing your dreams in an effective way—a way that will at once intrigue others, accurately inform them of your dream, and entice them to support you in achieving that dream. Being loud is about finding your voice and learning how to use it to share your story.

As for being proud? Well, being proud of your goals and dreams gives you the confidence you need to unabashedly announce them to the world.

Being loud and being proud are two different but highly connected and interwoven skills—and both are necessary to find the right community to support you on your way to achieving your dreams. The two skills build upon and strengthen each other constantly. In some instances you have to learn how to be proud of your dream before you can be loud about it. In other cases, being loud about your dream might help you gain the confidence to take pride in it. The saying "fake it till you make it" can often hold true: sometimes you have to believe in yourself and push forward, even when you have doubts about your path.

Everyone I've spoken to about chasing their dreams has struggled to some extent with the idea of being loud and proud. It can be really scary to talk about our dreams and put them out into the world for others to view and judge. And it can be hard to feel confident in and proud of our really big dreams, especially when they are so far away. Putting big, near-impossible dreams out into the world not only makes them seem more real—it also makes the risks of failure and rejection much more acute and scary.

But remember: one of the things that defines a dream is that it contains a goal that challenges you. And part of that challenge is being able to talk about it, even when that seems uncomfortable or scary. So let's talk about how exactly you can go about being loud and being proud, even when it's not your natural inclination.

 ## BECOMING PROUD

The cold, hard truth of the matter is that all of us experience self-doubt. In fact, it's often true that the more you care about and value something, the more doubt you feel about it. But here's the thing—doubt isn't necessarily a bad thing! Experiencing doubt can force us to view things more critically, to work harder, and to generally do better. That said, doubt can also stop us from even trying something in the first place, or cause undue stress and anxiety—and that's when it becomes a problem that has to be addressed. A little bit of doubt is good and very, very normal! But too much doubt—that's no good at all. Becoming proud of your dreams can help ensure that your natural self-doubt works for you, not against you.

To cultivate pride in your dreams, it's good to go back to what we talked about in chapter 1: passion. Remind yourself of why you are truly passionate about the dream that you are striving toward, and why you are completely, 100 percent, no-holds-barred dedicated to reaching that dream. Passion is *not* something that can be made up or faked, and thinking about why you're passionate about your dream can make it much easier to be both loud and proud about it.

The next step is to buckle down and do some research—and by some I mean *a lot*. Really dive in and learn everything you can about your dream. The reason it's important to do your research thoroughly is twofold. First, because your dream may entail a lot of nitty-gritty details that you hadn't known about before setting out to achieve it, and knowing the less-than-glamorous side of your dream and still being dedicated to it will increase your confidence. And second, having a deep base of knowledge about your dream will inherently increase your ability to be confident while talking to people about it, which in turn will help you feel more proud. I like to think of this as being overprepared so that you can over-deliver. There are lots of resources that can help you do this, and I'd recommend starting with the following:

☑ *Do some googling. When I was a kid, whenever I would ask my mom a question, she would say, "Google it"—and that was actually really good advice! The internet is chock-full of* information about just about anything. Find things to read that relate to your dream, including papers, blog posts, and both old and current news articles.

(✔) Visit your local or school library and see if they have any books or other materials related to the field that your dream is in. While you're at the library, make sure you talk to the librarian too! Librarians are there to help you navigate the library and find what you're looking for—and oftentimes they know about resources that you wouldn't even think to ask for!

(✔) Watch videos or listen to podcasts about your topic! Some of us learn better through reading, while others learn better through listening or watching. There are tons of great video resources and podcasts out there about pretty much every topic. Again, Google is your friend here! If you're having trouble finding resources online, whether they're articles, blog posts, or videos, ask an adult in your life to help you fine-tune your search.

(✔) Find an expert! Look for someone who is an expert in the field that you're interested in and see if they'd be willing to answer some questions for you. For example, if your dream is to be a varsity baseball player, find out who the local high school coach is and send them an email introducing yourself and asking if they could send you some information. (Check out chapter 8, "Mentorship," for more advice on contacting experts, and remember—whenever you're reaching out to talk to strangers, it's always important to have your parents/guardians help monitor your communications with them.)

Finally, a great way to become confident in your dream is by ensuring you have a plan in place for how to reach it. We'll dive deeper into the specifics of how to make a plan in the next chapter, but know that the research we talked about here will help you create a stellar plan to guide your dreams. For now, focus on learning as much as you can about your dream, finding out about how others have accomplished dreams similar to yours, and thinking about what it will take to get to your big dream. Just by taking these steps, your confidence in your dream will naturally start to grow, and you'll be well on your way to being as proud of it as you can be.

BECOMING LOUD

Once you've worked on developing pride and confidence in your dream, it's time to share this dream with the world. It's time to be loud. If you can muster up the courage to tell someone else about your dream—maybe starting with someone close to you who you think will believe in you and your ability to achieve your goals—that does two things. First, your confidant might be able to provide you some external support and belief in yourself.

Think of your trusted friends as cheerleaders for you and your dream. In the long run it is vital that you have internal confidence to fuel and support your dream, but it always helps to have external support as well! Secondly, telling someone else about your dream—just saying it aloud or seeing it written out—might help you believe in it more yourself. Sometimes we have to hear or see something to believe it's possible!

So how do you tackle being loud about your dream? Well, as with many things, practice makes perfect. I know, this phrase can be overused, but . . . it's also true. The best way to become comfortable and confident in talking about your dreams is to practice doing just that. Look for opportunities (or create your own opportunities) to share your dreams with the world.

For many of us, the easiest way to feel confident about talking about a dream is to tell someone we're close to about it. You can try this by picking someone who you believe will be supportive of what you're trying to achieve, like a parent, grandparent, aunt or uncle, sibling, godparent, teacher, coach, school guidance counselor, religious mentor, friend, or anyone else you feel comfortable around! Who you pick is totally up to you.

A great way to find people who you'll feel comfortable being loud and proud about your dreams with is to join clubs or groups that are based around your topic of interest. Peer groups are a great option because they're fun, nonthreatening, and a great way to find or build a community that will support your dream. And there are plenty of places to find them.

IF YOUR DREAM IS TO . . .	YOU COULD . . . - - - ▶
Be an actor, be on Broadway . . .	• Take an elective in your school's theater department • Try out for a school play • Join a local community theater or improv group
Learn to play an instrument, be a musician, become a rock star . . .	• Join your school's band or orchestra • Look for local musical jam sessions • Form your own band with your friends!
Learn how to paint or draw, become a professional artist . . .	• Take an elective art class at your school or at a local community center • Join an after-school art club • Get some friends together to create your own art, which could include anything from drawings of what you see in the world to a comic book that you all write and illustrate together
Learn to code, launch a rocket, or go into a STEM (science, technology, engineering, math) field . . .	• Join a local astronomy club • Join an after-school LEGO NXT robotics team • Join a Science Bowl team
Learn how to dance, look like a boss at the next school dance, be a professional ballet/hip-hop/modern dancer . . .	• Take a dance class • Join a dance troupe • Form a dance club with your friends
Write a book, get better and more comfortable with writing, be a writer or journalist . . .	• Join a writing club or book club • Get a group together to collectively do NaNoWriMo • Join your school's newspaper • Write a collaborative story with your friends

The options of types of peer groups you can join to both develop your skills and practice being loud and proud are nearly endless! A win-win way to find your crowd is by volunteering for a cause that's associated with your area of interest. And remember, if you can't find a club or group that fits your interests and your dreams, you can always start your own. Recruit your friends, post flyers on your school's bulletin boards or around your neighborhood, or post about it on social media. It's pretty likely that there are other people out there who are interested in the same things as you and would love to join a community dedicated to that interest.

Find Your Community!

You try it! Make a list of people who form your supportive community—like relatives, educators, friends, community members, and others—and then sort them into the diagram on the next page according to the categories they fit into.

Now that you've transferred your list of people into the appropriate circles, look at the center where all three circles overlap—which people fit in there? These are the people who you feel comfortable talking to, give good advice, and will be honest with you—essentially, these are the best people for you to talk to about your dream to practice becoming loud and proud!

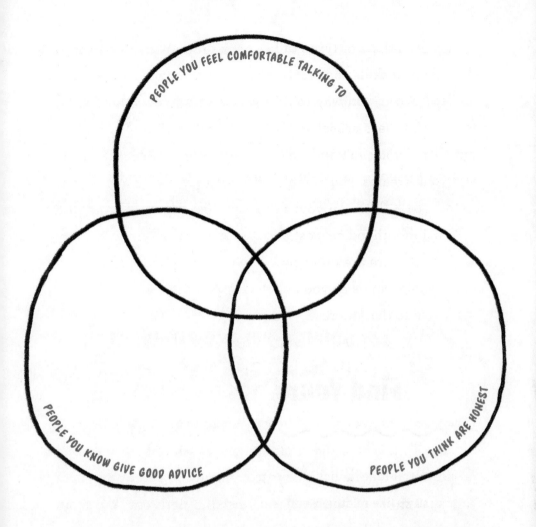

PEOPLE YOU FEEL COMFORTABLE TALKING TO

PEOPLE YOU KNOW GIVE GOOD ADVICE

PEOPLE YOU THINK ARE HONEST

Glory Edim is the founder of a book club turned worldwide movement called Well-Read Black Girl (WRBG). It all started in 2015 when Glory decided to be loud and proud about her passion by creating an Instagram account to highlight and celebrate literature by Black women. After seeing the hugely positive response to her page, Glory went on to start a WRBG book club and website, grew the WRBG social media accounts into a community with hundreds of thousands of followers, wrote her own book (*Well-Read Black Girl: Finding Our Stories, Discovering Ourselves*), and even launched a WRBG literary festival! Just like Glory, being loud and proud about your dreams and passions will help you find and create community, gain support for your dream, and overall feel empowered to reach for and chase after your dreams.

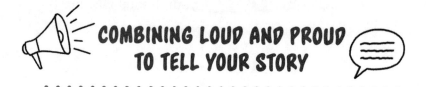

COMBINING LOUD AND PROUD TO TELL YOUR STORY

Now that you've figured out how to be proud and how to be loud, it's time to combine the two! The key to being both loud and proud at once is being able to communicate effectively about your dream—and to do that, you'll need to flesh out your story and cultivate your skill as a storyteller. Finding and telling your story is about speaking your truth in a way that isn't just factually accurate, but that also resonates with others. It's about finding a way to share what it is that you're passionate about in a way that other people can understand and appreciate, even if it's not what they themselves are passionate about. The goal is to help them understand both the thing you're passionate about *and* the reason behind your passion for, well, your passion. And hopefully, along the way, you can help them experience some passion of their own for whatever it is that you're talking about!

Your passions and dreams will likely seem very understandable and clear to you, but other people may not see them quite as clearly. It's possible that many of the people you talk to about your dream won't share your exact same passion—and as such, won't have your same interest in it or knowledge of it. So getting your passions and dreams across to others is all about good storytelling and crafting a compelling narrative to share your dreams with the world. But how do you do that in an effective way? It's all about choosing your audience, identifying your dream-specific vocabulary, picking your platform, and finding your story.

Choosing Your Audience

The first step in figuring out how to tell your story is to think about who you might want to tell it to. Who do you most value hearing about your dream and why? Who can help you achieve your dreams? Who do you have access to, and how can you gain access to people who you'd like to be in touch with but aren't currently? What kinds of help will you need to accomplish your dream and who can you get this help from? These questions can help guide you toward finding an audience to share your story— and your dream—with.

For me, my first audience was my immediate community.

From the age of about five until I was thirteen years old, I talked incessantly about my dream to anyone who would listen, including my mom, my teachers, and my friends. When I was thirteen, I branched out and started using social media to share my dream with the entire world. This allowed me to expand the community of people who were aware of and supporting my dream from just the specific people around me to the hundreds of thousands of people who now follow me on my social media channels.

Identifying precisely who it is that you're sharing your story with is incredibly important, because when you talk to someone about your dream you have to tailor what you're saying to suit the listener. By that, I mean that you want to be thoughtful about things such as:

 Not speaking at too high of a level—with lots of specific vocabulary, history, or complex concepts—for your audience to understand. And likewise, not telling your story with too narrow of a focus—without enough context or background information—for your audience to appreciate. For example, my dream is to travel to space, and even though I'll be the first person to tell you that I don't know everything about space travel, I do know a pretty decent amount. This means that I know more about space than most people in the general public who haven't learned about, heard about, or even thought about space travel since their sixth-grade science class. Because of this, it really wouldn't do much good for me to talk with most people in-depth about advanced orbital

mechanics, the chemistry of rocket propellant, or the specific engineering of space life-support systems. Discussing your passions at too deep of a level, or using obscure terminology and references, can alienate your audience.

(✓) *Switching up your tone and style based on your audience.* I've shared my story with pretty much every audience you could imagine—from preschool classes to the US Congress—and in doing so have learned that not every audience responds to the same tone and style. When I'm in a more official setting, such as giving a keynote speech, I aim for a more serious and businesslike tone. In less official settings, like a classroom or social media, I aim to be more conversational and relaxed. This includes the content I talk about, the tone of voice I use, and even my body language (for example, when I speak in kindergarten rooms I'll often sit on the floor with the kids I'm talking to—which is not exactly something I'd even think of doing in Congress!). No matter who you're talking to, what you're talking about, or what kind of platform you're using, nobody likes monotony!

(✓) Not oversaturating your audience by talking nonstop about your dream or in too much detail. Be aware of the interests of the person or people you are talking to and adjust your story to meet their interests. Allow your listeners time to respond to what you are saying!

Later in this chapter we'll dive into storytelling techniques that can help you create a compelling narrative about your dream. Learning how to tell a story about your dream will help you gauge who your audience is (their background knowledge, their interest, etc.) and talk to them at the right level.

YOUR DREAM-SPECIFIC VOCABULARY

Every dream has terms that are specific and unique to that particular dream. Unless the people you're talking to about your dream share your interest, it's likely that they won't understand *lots* of the specialized terminology and acronyms that seem totally normal to you! That can make it really difficult to share your dream with others.

For example, I frequently use terms like "Hohmann transfer orbit" and "Lagrange point," as well as acronyms like EVA, OMS, or CAPCOM. While these words make total sense to me and anyone else familiar with space travel, they wouldn't work for most people that I'm trying to talk to about my dream—to some folks, it might almost sound like I was speaking a different language! (In case you're curious, a Hohmann transfer orbit is the astrodynamic term for a maneuver in which a spacecraft switches to a farther orbit while using the smallest amount of fuel; a Lagrange point is a spot in space where the forces of two larger objects cancel out and allow a smaller object to remain motionless; EVA stands for extravehicular activity, which is the official name for spacewalks; OMS stands for orbital maneuvering system, which is what the miniature rockets that allow for spacecraft course correction are a part of; and CAPCOM is short for capsule communicator, which is the title given to the only person in mission control who's allowed to talk directly to the astronauts in space.)

Every dream has terms like this that are specific to the subject but gibberish to the rest of us. To participate in a professional ballet class, you have to know pretty much an entire dictionary of French-influenced words, such as "battement développé" (to extend the leg outward from the fifth foot position). To watch a game of football (and actually understand what's going on!) you'd need to know what a "halfback" is (the player who carries the ball while running longer distances). If you listen to a lecture about economics, you might hear acronyms you don't know, like GDP (gross domestic product, the economic activity of a country). Obviously these specialized terms and acronyms are useful while talking to people who understand them (just look at how many extra words I had to use to explain each of them!) but to most people . . . they're just confusing. Being aware of what specialized terms we use to talk or think about our dreams can help us avoid using them when talking to people who don't have a similar background on the topic.

Pinpoint Your Lingo

Now you practice—use the following journaling page to list any acronyms, words, terms, and phrases that you can think of that are unique to your dream!

PICKING YOUR PLATFORM(S)

Just as important to cultivating your story as choosing your intended audience is picking what platform you'll use to distribute your story. All this really means is asking yourself, "How do I want to communicate my dreams to others?" For some, this might mean simply talking about your dreams verbally with the people around you—like your family, friends, teachers, or coaches. You might also want to try public speaking, which you can start doing by talking to small groups like classes in your local elementary school or extracurricular clubs at your own school. Another option is to communicate your dreams by way of digital platforms like social media. In this day and age, the choices of how and where you can share your story are nearly endless.

To help choose your platform or platforms, start by asking yourself the following questions:

* *What do I hope to accomplish by sharing my story?*
* *Who is my intended audience, and how can I best reach them?*
* *What types of conversations or public presence am I comfortable with?*

Once you've figured out your answers, you can start to review which platforms fit for you. This is something that you can ask people in your community to help you with as well. Different platforms to be loud and proud on include public speaking, volunteering and public service, social media, events and conferences, and competitions. Each one of these can serve a different role in helping you speak out about your dreams.

Here's an example: if you find that speaking about your dream, even just to the people around you, is really fulfilling, then an avenue to consider is public speaking. An important thing to remember as you consider this is that your value as a public speaker is not tied to your age or even necessarily to your accomplishments—you don't have to have accomplished your dream already to speak about it! The only thing you need in order to make public speaking a great platform for you to pursue is to have a dream that the public will benefit from hearing about.

I started doing public speaking when I was about fifteen. I was working as the Earth liaison to an astronaut on the International Space Station, trying to share his experiences living and working in space with people here on Earth. One of the ways that I told people about his life in space was by speaking in classrooms, and then eventually at conferences (like TEDx). Speaking in schools was a great opportunity for me—both because I was able to expose a lot of young people to how awesome space is and because I was able to use the opportunity to develop my skills as a public speaker. If you think public speaking would help you share your dream with your community, I highly recommend starting small, in classrooms or after-school programs. All you need to do is reach out to school administrators or program directors and ask them if they'd be interested in hearing from you!

And just so you know, public speaking doesn't have to be scary or difficult. (I actually love it at this point!) You can get to a point where it's not nerve-racking simply by practicing frequently, and by starting with a group that is nonjudgmental. After speaking to lots of classrooms and many Skype calls with school groups around the world, I can now comfortably speak to groups of thousands of adults in all sorts of scenarios, including research conferences, congressional sessions, and even at the Kennedy Space Center. It's so helpful to start developing your abilities as a public speaker early, because public speaking can be an incredibly useful skill for many aspects of your future.

Another great way to develop your ability to share your dream with the world is by attending events or participating in competitions in your area of interest. Often the most valuable part of any event or competition isn't the event itself, or the competition prize, or anything else like that—it's the other people you'll meet while there! Going to events and competitions that are related to or focused on your passion can bring you into contact with lots of incredible people and resources in

your field that you might never find out about otherwise. A helpful hint is to network at all of the events you attend. This means meeting new people and making sure you get their contact info in case you want to reach out after the event ends. Events you might try to attend can include conferences, festivals, lectures, and readings. Additionally, you can participate in competitions that might help further your dreams, like the 3M Young Scientist Challenge, the Google Science Fair, National History Day, Model United Nations, and the Kids Philosophy Slam. Just like finding opportunities to speak publicly might take some legwork, you'll probably have to do some searching to find the right events or competitions to help you chase your dreams. To find events or competitions that are specific to your dream, try asking the people around you or looking online.

When you do find an event or competition that's exciting to you, make sure you prepare for it beforehand! Do some quick research about what the event has been like in the past, who else will be at the event, and so on. I guarantee that you'll get more out of any event or competition that you participate in if you go into it well prepared. And while you're at the event or competition, don't be afraid to be social! Oftentimes some of the most valuable things to come out of participating in these types of things are the people you meet and the relationships that you build.

And hey, being social doesn't mean you need to be the social butterfly who is working every part of the room. There are plenty of ways for extroverts *and* introverts to be social, such as:

✔ *Print simple business cards with your name, dream or area of interest, and email address and use these to open conversations with people when you meet them.*

✔ *View other students' work and ask questions. Showing interest is a great way to break the ice.*

✔ *Set up a Twitter account and follow the event hashtag, look for other students who are commenting on the event and reply to them (and follow them), share photos of your projects and others' and name and tag other students, and look for ways to connect online before meeting offline. Twitter is a great platform for introverts to use to get connected.*

On the digital media front, you likely already know at least some of what's available to you. Platforms where you can share your story might include iTunes and Spotify, where you can start a podcast or show; a blog-hosting site such as Medium, WordPress, and Tumblr, where you can share your written words; or Twitter, Facebook, YouTube, Instagram, Snapchat, TikTok, and others, where you can post pictures, articles, thoughts, videos, and more in a personal or professional way. None of these channels are inherently better than the others, but some might be better suited to you and your purpose.

A great way to determine which channel will work better

for you to share your dream on is to ask yourself what type of media will highlight it best. For instance, you can look at Instagram like a public photo album, so if your dream lends itself well to imagery, this might be the platform for you to use. Likewise, if you think your story will shine more vibrantly as a video, you can use YouTube; if a written piece seems more logical, Twitter, Facebook, or a blog site might be more your speed. Twitter, Facebook, and Instagram are all really great places to find and build community—they allow people to discover you easily and communicate quickly.

One important thing to consider if you choose to use social media to share your dream is whether you want to use personal or professional accounts. To share my dream, I chose to set up professional channels rather than using my personal ones because I wanted to keep my personal channels limited to the people I know personally (my friends and family) and also wanted to be sure that they weren't completely focused on space. I also realized that future employers might someday look at my professional accounts, and I wanted them to reflect a more serious and focused tone. The distinction between personal and professional channels is meant both to promote your dream through professional behavior and to keep you safe by protecting your personal information and life from the general public.

While talking about your dreams (whether by way of social media, public speaking, competitions, public service, or any other forum), safety should always be your first priority. Simple safety precautions like locking down your privacy settings on your social media channels, involving an adult in your public service activities, and never sharing personal information online or in person can help you stay safe. I started using social media to share my dreams with the world when I was thirteen years old, so of course, at that time, my accounts and digital communications were monitored by my mom. Even now, at twenty-two, as an influencer with hundreds of thousands of followers, I still ask my mom for help with reviewing my accounts!

FINDING YOUR STORY

Of course, to use storytelling as a means of communicating your dreams with the world, building a community, and finding help in reaching your dreams, you have to decide what your story is. And now that you've thought about who to reach out to, and which platform to use, it's time to figure out just how to shape the story you plan to tell. Before we even start to think about that, though, let's first define what your story really is. You can use the template on the next page to help with this process. Be as specific as possible!

Define Your Story!

Use this template to organize your story so you can effectively communicate with the world and gain support for your dreams! Fill out the template, then continue reading this chapter to learn how to craft your individual story.

What is your dream?

_____

Why does your dream matter?

_____

How does your dream connect/relate to the world?

_____

Does your dream affect others?

_____

When did you first discover your dream?

_____

How did you discover your dream?

_____

In the table on the next page, write down as many things as you can that have already happened to set you on the path toward your dream, as well as the top few goals that you have for the future to help you reach your dream.

PAST EXPERIENCES	FUTURE GOALS
1.	1.
2.	2.
3.	3.
4.	4.
5.	5.
6.	6.
7.	7.
8.	8.
9.	9.
10.	10.

Now take a look back at what you've just written down. See what themes, ideas, or experiences stand out to you—those are the elements that will form the core message of your story. By focusing on these ideas, you can start to craft a compelling story to share with people through speaking, social media, or whatever other forms you choose!

One of the most important features of effective storytelling is that it utilizes a broad spectrum of true emotions. This both keeps the audience engaged and helps relay the correct information to them. Think about how boring it would be to watch a movie, TV show, or web series where the actors all spoke in the same tone, with the same facial expressions, and with no body language throughout the entire thing. You would probably lose interest pretty quickly, and even for the parts that you were able to pay attention to, how much would you really understand of the plot? Emotion has been key to how we communicate for as long as we have been human—even before we developed speech—and as such, it holds a deep meaning to us, and its absence is noticeable.

As important as emotion is, on its own it's not enough to make a story worth telling—or make it worth your audience's time to listen to. If you truly want your story to be compelling and engaging, it's important that it does the following things:

★ *Educates your audience about your passion and dream*
★ *Is relatable even to those who aren't in your field*
★ *Is well organized*
★ *Is memorable*

So how do we go about incorporating all of these elements into the story we tell about our dreams? A great way to make sure that your story has all the necessary components is to plan how you'll talk about it and practice often. One of the best ways to plan and practice talking about your dream is to form it into something called an "elevator pitch."

Elevator pitches are short monologues. The name "elevator pitch" is based on the idea that you're stuck in an elevator with someone and you only have the time between when you both get in and when one of you gets out to describe and convince them of something. A typical ride in an elevator is only a minute or two long—so your elevator pitch needs to be just as speedy! Putting your story into such a concise format not only ensures that you can tell it to people without losing their interest, but also forces you to choose what's actually important for you to share.

The whole idea of elevator pitches is that they're super concise and yet hit all the important points. In a successful elevator pitch about your dream, you'd follow this easy format:

1. **State what your dream is.**

2. **State what you want your dream to accomplish.**

3. **State why your dream matters and how others can help.**

Remember: The whole point is to keep it simple, straightforward, and concise. But still persuasive! The following activity will guide you in writing your very own elevator pitch.

Craft Your Elevator Pitch

First, set a timer for five minutes. Write down everything you want your listener to know about you and your dream on the lines on the next page. At this point just let everything flow out—don't worry about brevity, clarity, or anything else! If you're feeling stuck, think about your answers to these questions to get started:

★ Who are you?

★ What's your dream?

★ Why does your dream excite you?

★ What are you doing (or planning to do) to achieve your dream?

★ What can your listener do to help you achieve your dream?

Once five minutes are up, read over what you wrote and mark

it up! Underline, highlight, or put a star next to any sentences or ideas that you think are super important, cross out anything that's repetitive or doesn't seem quite as important, and circle any words or phrases that might be confusing to a casual listener. Consider numbering your points based on how important they are or in what order you think they should go in your elevator pitch.

_____

_____

_____

_____

_____

_____

_____

_____

_____

Now that you've ruthlessly edited your story down to the bare bones, rewrite it. But this time write it in the box on the next page. Use only the most salient details: the whole point is to force yourself to ask—and answer—"What's *really* important to me and my story?"

When you're done, say your elevator pitch out loud a couple of times to practice! Often, the way that we write is slightly different from how we would normally speak, so it's okay to not read it word for word if a sentence structure or word choice doesn't feel natural to you. Try timing yourself to see how long your elevator pitch is. If it's more than a minute long, you'll need to cut some more stuff out.

Once you've written your elevator pitch, try it out on someone you trust to share your dreams with—start with someone close and comfortable, like your parent or sibling. Ask them for feedback, then write down what they said and use it to adjust the pitch for when you take it to your next audience. How did their reaction make you feel? How did talking about your dream out loud make you feel? Does it feel more in reach now that you have said it out loud?

Being able to tell your story well (concisely, understandably, and engagingly) is a super-important skill! Remember, *you* know why your dream is exciting and important, but most other people won't. Storytelling is how you involve others in your dream by engaging and educating your audience. Choosing your audience, identifying your dream-specific vocab, picking your platform, and practicing how to tell your story will help you be able to effectively talk about your dream and what you're doing to reach it with anyone you meet. This is a major tool in your "loud and proud" tool kit, and it'll help you build your community and propel your dream forward.

We all need a community—or multiple communities—to achieve dreams both big and small. Finding the right community to support you, and learning how to inform this community of your dreams and ask for the help you need, can be challenging. The solution to this challenge is to be loud and be proud. No matter how big your dreams may seem, speaking up and sharing them with the people around you can only improve your chances of reaching them. Talking proudly about our dreams to the people around us is the first step in finding community.

CHAPTER 3

When Rubber Hits the Road: Making a Plan— and Sticking to It

When I reach a goal I cross it off and set a new one.

—Katie Ledecky, record-setting Olympic swimmer

Now that you've defined your dream and started sharing it with the world, it's time to go about making it a reality! But before you can start chasing after your dream, you have to figure out *how* to do so. How can you most effectively strive toward your dream? Most dreams are not accomplished through one action or in one moment—instead, they are the result of a multitude of smaller actions over time, all of which combine and build toward a larger goal. To turn a dream from an abstract "maybe" to a concrete "definitely," you have to determine what all of these smaller actions should be and when (and how!) you'll achieve them. To put it simply, you've gotta *make a plan*! In this chapter I'll share with you how I made my own plan to achieve my big dream (and what's changed along the way!), dive into why making a plan matters so much, and walk you through how to make your very own step-by-step plan to reach your dream.

I made my very first plan to achieve my dream of becoming the first astronaut to walk on Mars when I was eleven years old. I had already spent several years being loud and proud about my dream, and eventually someone in my life heard me, believed in me, and stepped in to help guide me toward achieving it. My mom—my first and biggest supporter—challenged me to put together a plan of how I would go about accomplishing my astronomically challenging dream. She asked me to honestly consider how difficult it would be to take all of the steps that would lead up to me someday walking on the surface of Mars. It was the first time I'd thought about my dream in such concrete terms.

That night I dove voraciously into research. I searched for what past and current astronauts had done to become astronauts. I made a list of all the things that I thought would help me down the path of becoming an astronaut. Then I arranged those things in chronological order to show when and how I would achieve each of these smaller steps. I had my first plan, and it included multiple decades' worth of actions that I would need to take to someday walk on Mars. The very next day I brought my mom a written copy of this plan.

Despite the fact that much of what was on my very first plan ended up not being a part of my real path toward Mars, I will always be grateful that my mom challenged me to create it at such a young age. Creating this plan early on taught me how to plan for my future—a very necessary skill. Having a plan also helped me believe in my own ability to accomplish my dream, and helped me prove to others that my dream truly was achievable. Essentially, having a plan not only gave me a path forward toward achieving my dream, but also gave me confidence in myself and my abilities.

This first plan was a jumping-off point for me—the actions that I took as a result of this plan helped me focus on what was important in my journey at the time: excelling at school, participating in athletics, and sharing my dream with others. Because I had a plan of action, when I was loud and proud and shared my dream with others, they saw that I was serious. And because people saw that, they took *me* seriously, and presented me with amazing opportunities, like attending launches, special tours of space facilities, conferences, and more. I was able to meet incredible people who would later become mentors, and to have experiences that sharpened and directed the focus of my dream. All of my future plans, and subsequently, the actions I've taken over the past decade, are because I learned from that first plan how to chase after a dream.

Making your first plan (or if you've already made a plan, further refining your plan) is important. Making and following plans is a skill that will help you throughout your entire life and can be learned and improved, but only if you start somewhere and then work at it! And as it did for me, making a plan toward your dreams will help you gain confidence in that dream, discover exactly what you need to accomplish to reach your dream, and set you up to start taking actions toward success. Read on, and utilize the activities in this chapter, to start developing your skills as an organized dream go-getter!

MAKE YOUR PLAN!

The basic formula for making a plan is: do research, brainstorm the goals you'll need to accomplish to achieve your dream, break these goals up into smaller actions and steps, write it all out, ask someone else to help review it or review it yourself (or better yet, do both!), and finally, revise your plan as time goes by. That may seem like a lot of things, but don't worry, I'll break each of them down.

DO YOUR RESEARCH!

The *very* first thing to do as you start making a plan to achieve your dream is research! Search for anything and everything that can give you information on how to achieve your dream. Try to find out what materials or resources you might need and how you can get them, who can help you reach your dream, and what the requirements and recommendations are to get to where you want to go.

For example, if your dream is to be a competitive figure skater, your research might include reading about what previous and current professional skaters did on their path to success—how many hours a day they practiced, what types of sacrifices they had to make, what things outside of skating (such as dance

lessons or strength training) they did to support their training, and what their attitude or outlook was during their early years as a skater. You could also look for local competitions to enter and scholarships or grants to help fund your future advanced training.

The types of things you'll look for will vary depending on your dream, but the same basic questions remain no matter what your dream is: Has anyone accomplished this dream in the past, or done something close to it? How did they do it? What resources did they have that you might also need? How can you get those resources? Who can help you?

There are many ways to go about finding out what you need to know. A few methods might include:

(✔) *Looking online or at a library for information about how others have accomplished the same dream that you have. A great way to find this information is by making a list of those people and then reading their Wikipedia pages, looking for books about them, or reading their websites or blogs (if they have one!). While it can be interesting to look at people who accomplished your dream decades ago, in the interest of making your plan as relevant as possible, you're probably better off looking at recent examples.*

(✔) *Finding out about any requirements or recommendations that you're likely to come across on the way toward reaching your*

dream. (Requirements and recommendations can be different! For example, the requirements to be a NASA astronaut include good health, a master's degree in a related field, and a minimum of three years of work experience. But the recommendations, which most astronauts in the last couple decades have done, include working in remote/dangerous and high-stress environments, having flight or scuba experience, and getting advanced graduate degrees.) Requirements will form the base of your plan, and recommendations will help you fill it in more. Once again, the internet is your friend here!

(✔) Talking to people who are involved in the field your dream lies in. (For example, if you want to make the high school volleyball team, you could reach out to the team's coach or a current player and ask them some questions!) Finding people to talk to in your field of choice may seem challenging at first. Teachers, mentors, and parents can help guide you to find the right people to talk to.

List Your Goals!

Using your research (and what you already knew about your dream!), brainstorm a list of the things that you'll need to do to accomplish your dream. Start with all of the requirements, then move on to any recommendations, and finally, include anything that you think will give you an edge over others or will generally make your chances of achieving your dream even better.

REQUIREMENTS

1.
2.
3.
4.
5.

RECOMMENDATIONS

1.
2.
3.
4.
5.

EXTRAS

1.
2.
3.
4.
5.

BREAK YOUR BIG GOALS INTO SMALL STEPS

To become an astronaut, the list of actions I needed to take included things like attending a good university, becoming a scientist, and learning foreign languages. Each of these items could then be broken down into smaller goals. For example, attending a good university was dependent on getting good grades in middle and high school, taking advanced classes in math and science, getting high SAT/ACT scores, having a strong list of extracurricular activities, and being able to show a good history of volunteering. Each of these could then be broken down *even more* into smaller goals and steps, such as finding a tutor for subjects I was struggling in, planning out my class schedule every semester, studying and doing my homework on a regular basis, and more. The big idea here is to break your dream down into smaller component pieces, all of which will collectively add up to be the whole dream.

Oftentimes our dreams can seem almost impossible to us. When you're just starting out on the path toward your dream, it can seem really far away. But our dreams are definitely achievable! Creating a plan to achieve our dreams can help us untangle them and make them more approachable. Breaking down our big dreams into smaller steps helps us see how, exactly, they're achievable *and* helps us start taking actions toward accomplishing the seemingly impossible. When I was eleven years old and thinking about someday walking on Mars, that seemed like an insurmountable dream. It was so far out in the future and would require so much more than I was currently capable of—how would I ever go about achieving it? Where should I even start trying? Once I made a plan and saw the steps that I needed to take, including the steps that I could start with even at that age, all of these worries faded away. It was much easier to just think about what I needed to do to graduate high school and get into college than it was to think about my dream as a whole. I had a jumping-off point that seemed much more attainable at the time.

Break It Down!

Use the following activity to identify the different actions and smaller goals that make up each of the bigger steps in your plan. For this activity you'll need to go back to the last activity on page 76 and choose one of the steps that you brainstormed to use here.

Write the step/ goal that you chose:	My goal is . . . _____ _____
Challenge your- self to think of three smaller steps that you can break that goal into:	To achieve my goal I will . . . 1. _____ 2. _____ 3. _____
Make these smaller steps real by estimating the dates/times that you hope to start and/or finish each by:	I will start/finish this by . . . 1. _____ 2. _____ 3. _____

To create your plan, you should make sure that each of these component pieces you've identified are of the right magnitude— that they're reasonable. Think about each of these miniature goals as if they're a stepping-stone on the path toward your dream. A path is really hard to walk on if the stepping-stones are too far apart from one another; likewise, it's difficult to continue down the path toward your dream if the individual goals are too disconnected. Feel free to take some of these smaller goals and break them up into even smaller steps—whatever makes the path toward your dream seem more manageable and your dream appear more achievable to you.

One other important thing to remember: as you work on creating this plan, you'll want to include steps and goals of different sizes. If you make all of your goals too big, you'll fail to achieve them frequently enough to stay motivated (or maybe won't even be able to get started on them at all!). Conversely, if you make all of your goals too small or easy, then, even as you achieve each one, you won't feel like you're making progress toward your dream. It's important to have a good mixture of goals—some that make for low-hanging fruit and others that make you stretch a bit more.

Set SMART Goals!

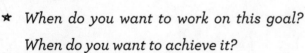

Having a plan with well-defined goals is super important. But if those goals aren't the right kinds of goals (as we just discussed above) you'll be setting yourself up for failure instead of success. Luckily, there's a handy acronym to help you set the right kinds of goals to achieve your dream: SMART goals! The acronym SMART stands for Specific, Measurable, Achievable, Relevant, and Timely. Let's break those five words down and look at what each of them actually means in terms of goal setting and dream go-getting!

SPECIFIC: Don't set vague goals—smart goals are well defined! You're much more likely to be successful at achieving your goals. To make any goal specific, make sure it answers these three *W* questions:

★ *Who does the goal involve? Is it just you, or does this goal involve others?*

★ *What exactly do you want to accomplish with this goal?*

★ *When do you want to work on this goal? When do you want to achieve it?*

MEASURABLE: Set goals that have measurable outcomes. It's easier to follow through on a goal if you can measure your progress toward it as you go. It's also much easier to feel empowered after you've completed your goal if you actively recognize when you've actually achieved it! Think of these things as ways to keep the mental momentum going. To ensure that your goals are measurable, ask yourself the following questions:

* *What criteria will indicate that you're making progress toward achieving your goal?*
* *What will achieving this goal look like? How will you know that you're done?*
* *Does your goal have times or dates attached to it?*

ACHIEVABLE: Your goals should be within your ability to achieve. If you set goals that are too big for you (right now), or too far in the future, you're setting yourself up to not achieve them! Setting *achievable* goals doesn't mean, of course, that you shouldn't feel challenged by your goals—they can be difficult, but still attainable.

RELEVANT: Make sure that you're setting your goals for a particular reason—smart goals should serve a purpose to you! To double-check that a goal you've set is relevant to you and your dream, ask yourself these questions:

* *Why are you setting this goal?*

- ★ *Why is it important to you?*
- ★ *How will it help you achieve your dream?*

TIMELY: Set goals that include start and end dates or times. Establishing goals that are set to be accomplished too far in the future (without intermediary goals or steps to break up that time) makes it less likely that you'll stay both motivated and organized to achieve them. Choosing time-bound goals also ensures that you can achieve them within the amount of time you have available! To ensure that your goals are timely, make sure that you have a clearly defined timeline for them, including how long you want to spend working on your goal, when you'll start working on it, and when you expect to achieve it.

Setting goals is a tool to help you achieve your dream! Planning out what you'll need to do (and how you'll do it) will help you feel motivated and empowered to go after your dream. Goals also help you focus on and determine what will actually help you succeed, and then use your time and resources to your best advantage. But like most tools, goals have to be used correctly to work. At best, incorrect goal setting will result in wasted time and effort—but at worst, it can negatively affect your ability to succeed and even cause you to lose your motivation and confidence in your ability to reach your dream. Utilize the SMART goals method to ensure that you're getting the most out of the goals you're setting so that the hard work that you do can help you achieve your dream!

Practice SMART Goal Setting!

Setting SMART goals is easier than it seems—and you can learn how to make SMART second nature when you set goals. As with anything, becoming proficient in SMART goal setting requires practice. Take a look at the list below, in which you'll find five not-so-SMART goals. Examine each one and in the space below it, rewrite it as a SMART goal!

1. I want to read more books.

_____

2. I want to become a better artist.

_____

3. I want to get drafted to an NFL team.

_____

4. I want to perform in the school musical.

_____

5. I want to save money for college.

_____

Now that you've practiced setting SMART goals, take a look at your own dream and set a SMART goal to help you reach it!

Write It Out!

By now you've determined the smaller component pieces that will help you start working toward reaching your dream, and it's time to actually write out your plan! Writing it out (rather than just thinking about it and keeping it inside your head) is super important. Oftentimes the action of writing something down (and then rereading it out loud) can help you find things you might have missed when you were keeping it all in your brain. Writing your plan down also makes it seem more tangible and real, ensures that you won't forget any of your smaller stepping-stone goals, and gives you something to look at to remind you of your bigger dream.

To create your written plan, organize all the ideas that you came up with during your research into chronological order. Determine which steps should come first, what's after that, and so on. Look at each of these steps and think about how you'll accomplish each one. Next to each step, write down anything that you think you'll need to have or do in order to achieve that specific step.

It's also a good idea to think about whether there might be anything that could stand in your way of accomplishing each step. The best way to not let obstacles get the better of you is by preparing for them beforehand! For each obstacle that you foresee, ask yourself how you think you'd react to it and whether there is anything you might be able to do to get around it. Some of these obstacles might never happen, but it's better to think about them and put together a plan B that you never have to use than it is to need a plan B and not have one. This is one of the incredibly powerful things about making a plan for your dream—it allows you to think more critically and at a more nuanced level about accomplishing your dream, and in doing so, to avoid and overcome obstacles that might stand in your way.

Of course, it's impossible to predict all the obstacles that might come along—life is unpredictable! It's completely okay (and normal!) to run into roadblocks and challenges while pursuing your goals that you didn't anticipate and that you're not prepared for. Here's the great thing though—preparing for potential future obstacles (even if you never end up facing the particular challenge you prepared for) will help you gain the skills necessary to deal with anything you encounter—even if the obstacle you run into isn't something you expected. Every dream that is worth doing is something that challenges you, and as such, will have challenging points along the way. You don't have to crumble under these challenges, and proper planning will help ensure you won't.

The most obvious, straightforward, and no-frills way to record your plan is to simply write it out, possibly on a piece of paper, in a notebook, or on a computer. These are by no means the only ways to create your plan though! If you think you want something a little bit more creative or interactive, consider these alternative ways to write out your plan:

(✓) *Write your plan out on a calendar! If your plan includes a lot of specific dates or if you really like the idea of keeping track of time while following your plan, this could be a great way to go.*

(✓) *Create a spreadsheet! This is a great option if you have a lot of moving parts to your plan. Creating a spreadsheet of your plan will allow you to record lots of extra information for each step, such as times, places, people, and more, and keep it all super organized. Spreadsheets are useful because they are customizable (Color-coding! Different fonts! Multiple pages and tabs!) and can be easily updated. Google Drive has a spreadsheet option (called Google Sheets) that is great for this type of planning, that is free, and that you can create a link from to share your spreadsheet with your mentors and advisors so that you can get feedback as you go.*

(✓) *Use sticky notes! Using sticky notes (like Post-its) allows you a lot of flexibility and creativity in your plan. You could write each individual step in your plan on a different sticky note, and then play around with color-coding them by timing, category, or any other classification that strikes your fancy. Sticky notes are great because you can put them anywhere, allowing you to keep whatever step you're currently working on front and center in your life. They also allow you to make changes easily. Did some-thing change in your plan? Just remove that sticky note and pop in a new one!*

☑️ *Use any other medium you find that excites you! Be creative—this is your plan, and how you record it is your choice.*

Once you've written out your plan, make sure that you display it somewhere prominently. Maybe print it out and paste it to the inside of your locker door, tape it up next to your mirror, or set it as your screensaver on your phone. Having your plan frequently visible will help you stay focused on your dream and its component pieces and will constantly remind you of just how achievable it is!

Katie Ledecky is an incredibly successful and highly decorated swimmer. By age nineteen, she had already been on the US Olympic team twice, won six Olympic medals, and won eighteen World Championship medals (the most of any female swimmer in the world!). She always keeps her goals prominently visible. While training for the 2016 Olympics, Katie had the numbers 565 printed on her pull buoy (a piece of training equipment swimmers use regularly). These numbers represented a set of goals she and her coach had decided on three years before the Olympics: to swim the 400-meter freestyle in 3 minutes and 56 seconds, and the

800-meter freestyle in 8 minutes and 5 seconds. Looking at these huge goals every time she trained helped Katie stay motivated and focused on achieving greatness. Just like for Katie, seeing your plan and goals frequently will help you stay focused and motivated to reach your dream.

GET A SECOND OPINION!

Once you've got your plan all figured out (or as figured out as you think you can get it) and recorded on your medium of choice, it's a great time to show it to someone else! Having a second pair of eyes look at your plan is important for any number of reasons. First, because you might be too emotionally invested in your work to look at it objectively, and you might miss something that someone who isn't as closely connected to your dreams would see. On top of that, someone else looking at your plan might notice individual parts that don't quite make sense, like steps that are out of order or not necessary at all. Conversely, they might be able to add in things that you hadn't even thought of yet!

An important thing to remember as you share your plan with other people is that it's still *your* plan. It belongs to you, and leads to your dreams, so you are the one who gets to make all the decisions regarding it. Other people can give you suggestions, constructive criticism, and advice, but at the end of the day you get to choose which ideas to include and which to dismiss. Not all advice that you get will fit for you, so don't feel pressured to change your plan based on someone else's opinion of it.

You can share your plan with anyone you choose, but a good thing to ask yourself as you're thinking about who the right person or people might be is: *Who do I think can give me good advice on this?* It might be helpful to go back to chapter 2 and think about who you first wanted to share your dream with and why you chose them. That original confidant might be a good person to give you your second opinion on your plan. Alternatively, if you have access to someone within the field that your dream is in, they might be a great person to share it with! For example, your theater teacher might be able to give you advice on what's realistic (or not) and what you might add to your plan that's specific to becoming an actor.

REVISE YOUR PLAN OVER TIME!

As you move ahead with your plan, you'll likely find that following it word for word isn't realistic. There are plenty of reasons why it might need to change. Your priorities could evolve, you could learn more about your dream and realize you need to add or subtract something from your plan, what (and who) you have access to might change, or the timeline for your stepping-stone goals might just shift. Whatever the reason, the important thing to remember is that nothing is set in stone. Just because you've written something down doesn't mean that that's the only way to do it. This is your plan and you get to follow it, or change it, as you'd like. A plan is meant to guide and support you, to help you engage in self-reflection. It's not meant to box you in!

My own plan that I laid out for myself when I was eleven included things like going into the air force and becoming an astrophysicist. It turns out that neither of these things was necessary to achieve my dream, and neither of them was really right for me. As I got older and continued to consider and refine my plan, I realized that I didn't want to go into the military. The next iteration of my plan included going to a large tech university like MIT to major in astrophysics instead. But after two years as an early college student (I was enrolled in college and high school at the same time) at a large university, I realized that what I actually wanted was to go to a smaller liberal arts college. And after having taken a couple of physics classes already, I was able to understand that my heart really wasn't in astrophysics. My plan then shifted once again, to me going to Wellesley College and studying astrobiology.

But I didn't only subtract or substitute things from my plan. I added components as well, based on learning new things about what would help me become an astronaut and discovering new resources that I had available to me. And so I added things like becoming a pilot and learning to scuba dive. Some things didn't change at all—I've always stuck with my initial ideas of becoming a scientist and learning multiple languages. Overall, the thing that changed the most about my plan was altering its timeline—sometimes moving certain steps up, other times moving steps further into the future. It just goes to show that none of us can predict the future, so as we plan for it we have to be willing to sometimes go with the flow and make changes to where we thought we were going and what we needed to be doing.

TAKE ACTION!

Making a plan is really only the first step (albeit an incredibly important first step!) in transforming your dream from a fantasy into a reality. After you've created your plan, after you've determined the path that you'll take and the individual smaller goals and actions that will help lead you to your dream, and after you've written it all down and shared it with others, you then have to start actually acting on those smaller goals. A plan on its own doesn't accomplish anything—it's just a list of ideas and timelines. It's the dreamer, not the plan, that achieves dreams.

As we've discussed above, making a plan to achieve your dream makes it much easier to just *get started* on working toward your dream. But even once you have a plan, once you've decided what you need to do to achieve your dream and broken it down into approachable steps, it can still sometimes be difficult to take the first step. Here are some skills and strategies that will help you get over the "getting started" hurdle and reach consistently toward your dream (even during the hard parts!).

Take That First Step

Are you familiar with the Nike tagline *Just do it*? Seems like good advice, right? Well, it's not always so easy to "just do it." Anyone who's ever started something new will tell you that the hardest part is the beginning—just getting started can be a huge task! It's completely okay and normal to not get started right away; allowing your ideas to ferment and mature before you act on them is great. But eventually there comes a point when you do have to act on your dreams if you ever want to achieve them. If you've done your research, made your plan, and are still not totally confident in getting started, then it's time to turn inward and ask yourself why you're struggling.

We tell ourselves all sorts of stories about why we're not acting on our dreams: "It's not the right time," "I'm not ready," "I don't have the right resources to start," "I'm too busy," "It's too hard," and more. But the truth is that the main reason we avoid starting down the road toward our dreams is often because we're afraid. Getting over fear and self-doubt can totally be difficult (there's actually a whole chapter later on with more advice about overcoming fears!), but it's a necessary thing to do if you want to act on your dreams.

Oftentimes our trepidation and anxiety about starting down the path toward our dreams comes from uncertainty. Maybe we're not quite sure what exactly will happen if we start to act on our dreams—both the negative and positive results. The ability to overcome our fears or worries about taking action toward our dreams is based in becoming self-aware. Once you know why you're worried, it's much easier to look at that fear truthfully and not let it control you!

Take the First Step Toward *Your* Dream!

One great way to take your first step is to start with the easiest or quickest step in your plan. Some plans have to be followed in a certain order, but most have at least a little bit of flexibility. Starting with something that you can accomplish quickly is smart for two reasons. First: a really quick and easy task is probably less scary to think about doing, and therefore easier to, well, just do! Second: actions, even small actions, build momentum and confidence; once you've accomplished one small task, it's easier to look at the rest of your steps and feel like you can achieve them too.

You're probably familiar with the name Sir Isaac Newton. Newton is one of the most well-known and famous scientists in all of history—and for good reason! Over three hundred years ago he discovered gravity, invented the mathematics of calculus, and identified the three laws of motion (known as Newton's Laws of Motion). These three laws are fundamental to our understanding of modern physics—and especially important if you want to understand high-speed activities such as racing cars, launching rockets, and flying airplanes! Newton's first law, also known as the Law of Inertia, states:

An object at rest will remain at rest unless acted upon by an outside force; an object in motion will remain in motion unless acted upon by an outside force.

This law is intended to describe the actions of physical objects—but you can also apply it to the actions that you take to reach your dream! Let's go ahead and change the statement of Newton's first law to describe your plans instead:

1. The *object at rest* = your plan to achieve your dream, before you start on it
2. The *outside force* = taking actions toward or away from your dream (i.e., following the steps of your plan or disregarding them)
3. The *object in motion* = your plan, once you start working on it

So now Newton's first law [for your dream] states:

Your plan (at rest) will remain at rest unless you take actions toward your dream; your plan (in motion) will remain in motion unless acted upon by an outside force.

Taking the first action toward your dream (no matter how small that action may be!) acts as the outside force to push your plan into motion. And once your plan is in motion it remains in motion—it has *inertia*! With this inertia already started it should be easier to continue acting toward your dreams, allowing you to undertake some of the bigger, more difficult steps in your plan.

As you get started acting on your plan, please be kind and patient with yourself! Just getting started is a huge accomplishment and something to be proud of, regardless of how long it takes you or how successful you are with your first action. Acting on your plan is a skill and something that you shouldn't expect to be perfect at right away—but over time you can (and will!) get better at it.

OVERCOMING PROCRASTINATION

Procrastination is something that everyone faces at some point or another. Maybe you'll procrastinate to avoid getting started on figuring out a plan for your dream (if so, see the section on page 93 called "Take That First Step"), or perhaps you'll procrastinate after you've started down the path toward your dream. Dreams are exciting, and chasing them should be something you enjoy, but that being said, you probably won't enjoy every moment of every step on your way! Some of the actions that you take to accomplish your dream might be boring, difficult, or otherwise unpalatable in some way, and that can lead to procrastination. While procrastination is a normal experience, it doesn't have to be something that stops you from chasing after your dream—overcoming procrastination is not as hard as it seems, and you can absolutely learn how to do it.

One important thing to remember: procrastination is not the same thing as laziness! Procrastination is when you focus on doing things other than the task at hand—oftentimes the alternative activities that you partake in when you procrastinate are easier to do, quicker, more fun, or somehow more appealing than the one you are procrastinating doing. Another important thing to keep in mind is that procrastination is a habit. Every time you procrastinate, you reinforce the likelihood that you'll procrastinate again in the future—so it's important to nip it in the bud! Dealing with procrastination starts with the obvious: recognizing and identifying when you're procrastinating. If you realize that you're not getting something from your plan done that you should have finished by now (or even should have just started), then you might be procrastinating. If you think that might be the case, go ahead and ask yourself these questions:

Am I purposely avoiding doing [whatever it is that I should be doing]?

Am I really too busy to do [this particular thing] or am I filling my time with less important things to avoid it?

How long has [this thing I should be doing] been on my to-do list?

Am I making excuses for why I haven't done [this thing I've been meaning to do]?

If you answered yes to any of these questions (or maybe even to several of them) then you are probably procrastinating...

Once you've identified that yes, indeed, you are procrastinating, the next thing to do is to figure out *why* you're procrastinating. It's important to figure out the why before you start trying to fix it, because different reasons for procrastinating have different solutions! Picking the right solution for your procrastination will make it much easier to stop. Try to identify whether you're procrastinating on your task because you find it boring, unappealing, or difficult; because you're worried about failing at the task; because you're struggling with organization; or for some entirely different reason.

Once you've figure that out, it's time to start working on stopping the procrastination. Here are some anti-procrastination strategies that I've found effective. Feel free to try out different strategies until you find one that works for you (or go ahead and combine multiple strategies if you think that'll work best!):

✓ **Commit yourself to your task.** *You might be procrastinating because you're not really, truly committed to the task that you're trying to accomplish! Ask yourself why you're trying to accomplish this particular task—what will achieving it do for you? Do you really want to achieve it? If the answer is yes, make a mental commitment to yourself to do so. Then make a physical commitment as well. Write out your task on a piece of paper in* big letters and put it in front of you. Make it look important and eye-catching—even go as far as to decorate it if you want! If it's something that will take you a while to do, put this paper in a place where you'll see it frequently.

(✔) **Give yourself a timeline** to get started or finished with your task. Choose a date or time that you want to have either started or finished your task by and then set an alarm to remind you to do it. My favorite way to do this is to use a countdown clock from TimeAndDate.com/Countdown/Create. I love using this site because it lets you create a customized background design, title, and date/ time for your goal. You can then either keep this open on your phone or computer, or check back in on it and watch as it counts down to your deadline!

(✔) **Create short bursts of time for yourself.** Choose a small amount of time, set a timer, and then work on your task for that much time. You'll probably find that it's easier to get started on your task when you've promised yourself that you only have to do it for a short amount of time—and you might even find that, once you've started, you'll be able to go longer than you expected. For example, when I'm training for a long-distance race, sometimes I know I should go jogging but just really don't feel like doing it. I deal with this by starting to run, and setting a timer for just five minutes to start with. (*My logic here is that I can do anything, even if I don't want to, for five minutes. Feel free to choose your own amount of time to use!*) When the timer goes off, I'll have gotten into the groove and often decide to keep running for another five minutes, and then another . . . and eventually I'll stop setting the timer and just run!

(✔) **Become organized about this particular task.** *Choose a period of time in the near future that you will block out to work on your task. Plan to minimize the distractions around you during this block of time. (For example, make sure you have study snacks easily accessible, a quiet space, and no access to social media.)*

(✔) **Reward yourself** *(or plan to!) for accomplishing your task. What you consider to be a reward depends on you and what you like, but some examples are: playing a video game, eating a piece of chocolate, crossing your task off your to-do list or plan, or telling someone (or posting on social media) once you've accomplished your task.*

(✔) **Find an "accountabilibuddy."** *In case it's not clear, that word is a mash-up of "accountability" and "buddy," and it's someone who will help you make sure you stick to your task! You can ask a friend, family member, team member, teacher, or anyone else that you're close to to be your accountabilibuddy. Ask them* to check in with you at a predetermined time—maybe a couple hours, maybe a couple days—to ask you whether you've started, finished, or reached a certain point in your task. Sometimes accountabilibuddies can be people with the same task who work on it together and motivate each other.

(✔) **Change your mindset** and the words that you use when you think of or talk about your task. Challenge yourself with this! If you constantly use words with a negative connotation when you think or talk about your task, then it will start to seem like a chore that you have to do instead of something that you're choosing to do. Use the next activity to help make this mindset shift!

YOU GOT THIS!

Shift Your Mindset Away from Procrastination!

Check out the words and phrases on the next page, which are frequently used when thinking about a task. Circle the ones you use in your own internal dialogue when you think about the task you're trying to get done.

I need to do . . .	I choose to do . . .
I have to do this . . .	I can do this . . .
What a boring task . . .	This task is important to me . . .
This is going to take forever . . .	I'm excited to dive in deep and do this in a quality way . . .
I should have already done this . . .	Now is a good time to start . . .
This has to be perfect . . .	This is just a start; it can be imperfect . . .
Can't . . .	Can . . .
Have to . . .	Want to . . .
Failure . . .	Opportunity . . .

Use the space below to write down the types of words and phrases that you want to use when you think about or talk about the steps and tasks on your plan!

_____

_____

_____

_____

_____

_____

_____

Regardless of why or how often you procrastinate, please be kind to yourself as you work to recognize and change this habit. Remember that everyone procrastinates at some point. Struggling with procrastination does not mean that you're not capable of achieving your dream or following your plan—it's simply a challenge for you to overcome along the way. Be proud of yourself for being self-aware enough to notice your bad habits and dedicated enough to work on changing them!

ACT WITH CONSISTENCY

If you want to see the smaller, more actionable steps in your plan build upon one another to help you reach your dream, you have to act consistently on your plan. This means that you can't tackle the entire list of steps in your plan all at once—and neither can you leave huge gaps between tackling each step. You have to find a happy medium (like Goldilocks!). The following section will guide you in how to find your own Goldilocks zone for your dream.

Consider this: Is your dream a marathon or a sprint? Sprints and marathons are both running races but are fundamentally different activities, and as such, need different strategies. A sprint is a short-distance race, and in it you want to run as fast as you can for the entire race. If you were to treat a marathon like a sprint, though, you would probably collapse after the first couple of miles! In a marathon, which is 26.2 miles long, a runner usually starts out with a slower warm-up period and then runs at a consistent pace that they know they can maintain for the entire race.

In the same way that there are different strategies for runners to employ to be successful in various types of races, you'll also need to modulate your strategy for your dream based on how long-term and effort-intensive it is. If your dream is something that you can accomplish quickly (such as learning how to do a cartwheel), then you don't have to worry about pacing yourself very much. Feel free to tackle it at full speed! However, if your dream is something that you expect will take a longer time period to accomplish, then you'll need to treat it more like a marathon and pace yourself with consistent actions over time. For example, when I first dreamed up my dream to walk on Mars, I was planning for something that was thirty-plus years in my future! If I had dedicated 110 percent of my time and energy to achieving this dream, I would have burned out long before the thirty years were up.

To avoid burning out before you reach your dream, act with consistency as you reach for it. One simple way to do this is to review the plan you wrote out previously and ensure that you include in it a realistic timeline for when you plan to achieve each step. What exactly does "realistic" mean in this case? Well, for each dream (and each list of steps) this will be different! Here are some tips to help you figure out what the most feasible time-line for your dream might be:

✓ *If other people have achieved the same or a similar dream in the past, look at how long it took them to do so and how they paced themselves.*

✓ *Review your plan step by step and think about how long it will take to accomplish each one. Keep in mind that it's very likely each step won't need the same amount of time.*

✓ *While acting on your dream quickly is important, don't feel like you have to make your first action a massive one! Don't plan to go too far or too fast right off the bat. Choose an action that seems achievable. Review your plan to make sure that all of your steps are broken down into smaller steps that are truly action-able. (It's important and good to have stretch goals in your plan, but make sure that you have a plan of smaller actions to reach those stretch goals.)*

✓ *Plan to work on just one step at a time. Do the best job that you can on this one action and then move on to the next one once you've completed it. If you focus your attention on multiple steps simultaneously, you run the risk of not being able to commit enough attention to each of them individually and end up not achieving any of them in the long run!*

✔ *Once you've put a timeline into your plan, ask someone to review it and to specifically look at how reasonable your timeline is.*

Tips for Acting with Consistency

Once you have a well-thought-out, realistic timeline as a part of your plan, do your best to actually stick to it! To do so, here are a few helpful points to consider: *maintaining proper time management, building good habits,* and *overcoming inflection points.*

There are 24 hours in a day, 7 days in a week, and approximately 4 weeks in a month—so that means you have about 672 hours every month to work on your plan, right? No, of course not! You still need to sleep, eat, get dressed every day, go to school, participate in extracurricular activities, do homework, do your chores, read this book, hang out with friends, and many other things. Those 672 hours disappear *really* quickly once you start to think about all of the things you do. So how are you going to find time in your busy life to consistently act toward your dream? Well, that's where having good time-management skills comes in handy! Mastering those will help you organize your life, do all of your other tasks and activities more efficiently, and make time to work toward your dream.

Time management is all about determining what your

priorities are, how much time you have available, and how much time you want to allocate to each task, and then actually sticking with the choices you made. So the obvious first step here is to determine what your priorities are. At this point you might ask: Isn't everything in your life (and on your plan) important? Yes, which is why you have to think really critically about what your priorities are. Some things that you spend your time on seem important in the short term (like painting your nails or playing video games with your friends), whereas other things will be important to you in the long term (like achieving your dreams, doing well in school, or nurturing your relationships). What seems important to you today might not seem so important in a few weeks, months, or even years down the road. As you try to decide what to prioritize above all else, ask yourself, *If I looked back on this task a year from now, would I consider it to be important?* If you answer yes, then that task is probably an important thing and you should prioritize it!

Start by allocating as much time as you need to these important tasks, and then use the time that's left over to complete your less important tasks. If you're still not entirely sure which tasks are the most important, ask yourself, *What would happen if I didn't accomplish this task?* If there are no consequences, or very minimal consequences, then it's probably not a top priority for you. Consider this example: Your dream is to buy your own car when you get your driver's license. Right now you have a three-hour period of time that you can use however you'd like—you could either spend it watching a movie or spend it doing something like babysitting or mowing lawns to earn

 money. If you ask yourself what the consequences of NOT doing each of these would be, you'll pretty easily see which should take priority.

If you have multiple tasks that all seem to be really important (and will be important in the long run!) you can use the principle of urgency to decide what order to do them in. Ask yourself, *Do my tasks have due dates?* If only one of your tasks has a date it has to be accomplished by, start with that one! If they all have due dates, arrange them by which due dates are coming up first, and how much time each task will take to accomplish, and then plan your time based on that list.

Another way to keep a consistent pace when acting toward your dream is to incorporate habits into your plan. Habits can be incredibly powerful! Much of human behavior is based on habits—they control our everyday actions, oftentimes without us even knowing it. Decisions like what to eat for breakfast, when to brush your teeth, and even how you tie your shoelaces aren't actually decisions, they're habits. Habits make our lives easier by removing the need to make decisions constantly. And they're especially helpful for things that are difficult for us to choose to do otherwise. Humans have a limited amount of willpower, so relying on your willpower to keep you acting consistently toward your dream (especially during the more grueling parts of your path) is not a great idea. Instead, rely on making it a habit to work on your goals!

The final piece of the puzzle to stick to your plan and timeline is to anticipate and overcome inflection points. Inflection points are moments when the temptation to quit is the strongest, and regardless of what your dream is, you're bound to run into them at some point! Overcoming inflection points is all about thinking ahead about what, when, where, and why you might struggle and making plans for how you can instead succeed in those instances.

Oftentimes the inflection points that we face arise because the action we're doing is boring, monotonous, or otherwise unpleasant. Our brains crave variety, and if we're not giving them enough they rebel. In cases such as this, the best way to plan for success at these inflection points is to think of creative ways that you can make that difficult action or moment fun instead of it being a drag. For example, if your dream is to run a 5K but running becomes boring to you after a while, some things you could do to keep it interesting include changing up where you run so that the scenery is exciting; challenging yourself to run faster or go longer; listening to a podcast, audiobook, or movie while you run; or running with a friend! The way that you make your inflection point interesting will vary based on what the action you're undertaking is, but the basic idea is: Can you give your brain a more exciting environment or experience while still accomplishing the same task?

Make It Fun!

Use the following journaling activity to overcome inflection points successfully by planning ways to make your boring tasks more fun and interesting. You can think of this like a mental boredom bag that you keep with you all the time—but instead of packing your Switch, your favorite book, or a drawing pad, you're packing ideas!

Think about the list of steps that you'll need to take to accomplish your dream. Pick one that you think you might struggle to accomplish because of monotony or boredom and write it here:

_____

Now let's think of some ways to make that task more interesting!

★ How long do you think it will take you to accomplish your task?

_____

★ Our brains LOVE competition, even when it's just against a clock! Set yourself a goal for the fastest you think you could accomplish your task: _____

★ Where do you have to be to do your task? Sometimes just changing our scenery can provide enough variety to motivate us to enjoy something that would otherwise be boring. If you can be flexible in terms of the location you need to be in to accomplish your task, brainstorm three alternative places you could be to do it. Circle the one you think would be the most interesting or most fun!

1. _____

_____

2. _____

_____

3. _____

_____

★ How can you use all of your senses to make the task more interesting and engaging? Brainstorm a list of three things you could
do to add stimuli to your task—try to think of an idea for three
out of the five senses.

1. _____

_____

2. _____

_____

3. _____

_____

One of the great things you can do with your plan once
you start acting on it is to keep track of how far you've come. As
you work on a specific goal, highlight it or bring it to the forefront. And once you accomplish each small stepping-stone goal,
reward yourself by crossing it off your plan. Look back at your
plan every now and then to see how much progress you've made
toward accomplishing your dream—I promise you, you won't be
disappointed!

CHAPTER 4

Disrupting—an Essential Part of Success

I always thought this was for other people, and I was not qualified. There was this wake-up call of, Why not me?

—Chrissy Houlahan, congresswoman in the United States House of Representatives

Big change sometimes happens without us even intending it. The mere act of chasing a dream can create a cascade of change! When I first decided that I wanted to become an astronaut and go to Mars—and furthermore, that I wanted to share that journey (as a proxy of sorts) with everyone on Earth—I didn't say to myself, "I'm going to shift the way things are done by doing the impossible." I didn't say to myself, "I'm going to break stereotypes about women in STEM fields." And I definitely didn't say to myself, "I'm going to become a leader and an advocate for my generation." No, all I said was, "I'm going to follow my dream." Little did I know that the simple act of having and chasing a big dream would lead me on a path to becoming a public figure, an advocate for STEM education (and especially access to STEM for girls and minorities), and a leader in the future of space exploration.

One thing that many dreamers have in common is that they shift the status quo just by pursuing their dream. Seriously—think of so many of the people you know of who have successfully accomplished their dreams and ask yourself, *Did they play entirely by the rules of society?* I guarantee you, in so many cases, that the answer is no. Most of the people we hold up as icons and role models, the biggest dreamers and doers throughout history and up until today, didn't set out to make waves or change the world. From tech moguls to social justice heroes to world leaders, they all had dreams that they were following. These people were disruptors—society changers, paradigm shifters, standard setters—and their dreams were the vehicles they used to make waves. Dreaming and disrupting are naturally woven together, and as such, every dream, and every dreamer, has the potential to change the world.

So what does it really mean to be a disruptor? To be a disruptor means that you are willing to risk failure to push for change. Disruptors are willing to step outside of the status quo and do things in a different way, one that may challenge conventional and traditional thinking. But disruptors don't do this on their own; they work to bring others along with them, to create leaders, and to help drive forward the change they see as necessary for the future. Disruptors are often aware that bringing big ideas forward and getting people to think in new and different ways requires a village of people willing to join in the pursuit of something bigger than themselves. Being a disruptor can also mean creating your own opportunities when none exist. Ultimately, disruptors encourage social change, push for shifts in the public mindset, and can even lead cultural movements.

Sometimes being a disruptor is as simple as working in a field that hasn't traditionally or historically been open to you because of gender, race, or any other factor. Disruptors are pioneers of culture, invention, technology—in pretty much any field you can imagine, someone had to lead the way to make advancements, and those pioneers were all disruptors, each in their own way. Many of those who we now call disruptors earned that label by looking at seemingly impossible things and asking not only *Why not?* but specifically *Why not me?*

Chrissy Houlahan was one of those people who said *Why not me?* and went on to become a disruptor. Over the course of her life, Chrissy worked as an engineer in the air force, a top-level manager for both a sportswear company and multiple nonprofit organizations, and a high school science teacher. All of this was before she said *Why not me?* and pivoted her career—and her life—in a completely different direction. In 2017, Chrissy helped organize a bus to take people to the Women's March, the largest protest in US history, which fought to bring women's issues to the forefront of society and politics. It was during this process of organizing and attending the Women's March that Chrissy decided to take matters into her own hands—she was going to run for office. And she wasn't going to start small either— knowing that she was highly qualified and capable, Chrissy decided that, even though she'd never run for office before, her very first race would be for Congress. Chrissy said *Why not me?* and then went on to win, becoming the first Democrat in over 150 years to represent her district of Pennsylvania in the US House of Representatives. Just like Chrissy, no matter where you are in life, you have the ability to be a disruptor—and saying *Why not me?* might be the first step in doing so.

In the past, the role of disruptor was most often filled by adults and established professionals. Making change requires resources—resources most commonly attained by those with experience. But we are currently living in a new era, thanks to the internet, when young people have greater resources, including (but certainly not limited to) a voice, an audience, and vast communities. Today's youth—you, me, and all of our friends and peers—are empowered by the very technology that past generations of disruptors pioneered. We can leverage the digital world we were raised in to make serious and powerful change. And it's fortunate that we have such great ability to enact change, because our generation is facing unprecedented issues. Global climate change, drastically growing populations, pandemics, and decreased food and water security in certain regions of the world are just a few of the problems we're facing, and they make disruptors and the movements they lead more important than ever. Thankfully, instead of simply taking a gloom-and-doom attitude, a record number of young people are tackling social change and becoming leaders both in their generation and across generations, throughout the entire world.

It's pretty easy to see why we, as dreamers, should care about and think about disrupting. Whether or not you mean to, whether or not you decide to, and whether or not you even notice that you are doing so, following your dream can help you change the world! In this chapter we'll explore the stories of some of the most impactful historical and modern dreamers turned disruptors and see how their dreams led them to make a difference—then we'll look at how you, as a dreamer, can do the same.

FROM DREAMER TO DISRUPTOR !!/

So many of history's greatest disruptors—not to mention those who are still alive and kicking today—started out just like you and me: as dreamers. The mark of dreamers turned disruptors is ever present in our lives, even though we may not always realize it. Many of the technologies that we use on a daily basis (things like smartphones, laptops, fitness trackers, Bluetooth, AI assistants, and so many more) are a direct result of people who dreamed of making technology smaller, faster, smarter, more accessible, and all around just plain better. These tech whiz kids (think Microsoft cofounder Bill Gates, microphone designer James West, and Hedy Lamarr, a Hollywood actress who invented a radio signal that helped US forces during World War II) set out to reimagine what technology could be, instead of accepting it as it currently was. In doing so, they created some of the largest and most fundamental shifts in human culture worldwide. Similarly, visionaries such as the Wright brothers (inventors of the world's first successful airplane), Karl Benz (the inventor of the first gasoline-powered automobile), and Stephanie Kwolek (the inventor of Kevlar—a super-strong material that is nowadays used in tires, sails, airplanes, and even spacecraft!) all started with dreams and ended up permanently changing the world. These dreams drove them to think way outside the box and to develop impossible-seeming transportation technologies, and by doing just that, they became disruptors.

Because of the legacy of dreamers turned disruptors such as these, we now live in the most connected world (both digitally and physically) ever, a world that allows humans to engage, collaborate, and create like never before. So the big question then becomes: What exactly is it about dreams—and the people who chase after them—that makes them such agents of change? *Why* do dreamers become disruptors? *How* do dreamers become disruptors? Read on to learn about some of the coolest dreamers turned disruptors out there, and to see how chasing after your dream puts you in good company as a current dreamer and future disruptor.

WHY DO DREAMERS BECOME DISRUPTORS?

Many disruptors start off as dreamers chasing after their dreams, and in the course of doing so, happen upon their chance to make a larger difference in the world. By simply pursuing their dreams, many dreamers discover not only their voice, but their ability to impart lasting change. Dreamers become disruptors based on their understanding of the very nature of a dream, which, as we've said, is something that you want with all your heart, that you are willing to work hard and sacrifice to achieve, and that you truly believe in. Dreamers have the will and the drive to continue on when the going gets tough, to persevere and to change the way things have always been done, to look for something better and then make it happen. Their passion for their dreams leads dreamers to innovate and create their own opportunities when none are available to them or when those available aren't good enough. Solving problems or coming up with new ideas when the going gets tough leads to disruption. At the end of the day, disruption is a way for dreamers to make their dreams, skills, and privileges into something greater than themselves—a legacy.

A dreamer turned disruptor who truly showed how the drive behind a dream can change the entire world was mathematician Katherine Johnson. Katherine loved—and was very talented at—math for her entire life. Growing up as a Black woman in West Virginia in the early twentieth century, she faced—and overcame—immense obstacles as she pursued this passion because of the color of her skin. Katherine graduated early from high school and entered college at fifteen, and then, after getting an advanced degree in math, went on to work for NACA (the predecessor to NASA) as a computer (which at that point in history was the job title for someone who did mathematical computations—this was before digital computers were invented!).

During her time at NASA she worked on guiding and controlling the trajectory of spacecraft. Katherine didn't just do the math though—she pushed for things to be different. She gained a reputation for wanting to understand things fully and constantly asking questions, for having novel ideas about how things could be done, and for pushing against the boundaries that society had placed on her. Because of her excellence at her job, and because of the waves that she had made, Katherine was an integral member of the space program as a whole, and particularly of the Apollo program, which sent humans to the moon. It was Katherine who, in 1961, calculated the trajectory for the flight of the very first American in space, astronaut Alan Shepard. And it was Katherine who, in 1969, became the person who checked and confirmed the trajectory calculations for Neil Armstrong and the very first moon landing!

The Apollo program not only allowed humanity to walk on an extraterrestrial body, it also shaped the world that we know today. The massive challenges NASA faced in sending astronauts to the moon, landing them on its surface, and bringing them back to Earth, combined with the massive budget they got to achieve this, resulted in unbelievable gains in technology, science, and space exploration that continue to impact our lives on a daily basis. Katherine never set out to change the world, but her work on the Apollo program solidified her legacy as a dreamer turned disruptor whose passion, tenacity, and innovation shaped the world we live in for generations.

Another dreamer turned disruptor who embodied the very nature of dreaming—and how dreaming big gives you the drive to push through obstacles—was US Supreme Court Justice Ruth Bader Ginsburg (sometimes referred to as the Notorious RBG). Justice Ginsburg was the second woman ever to have been appointed to the United States' highest court. Her career as a lawyer, professor, and Supreme Court justice was strongly and very visibly impacted by the many obstacles she faced in her early years of striving toward her goals. As early as her first year of law school, the deck was stacked against her success. As one of only nine women in a class of about five hundred at Harvard Law School in 1956, Ginsburg faced massive prejudice and sexism. It went as far as the dean of Harvard Law explicitly asking her and each of her eight fellow woman students, "Why are you at Harvard Law School, taking the place of a man?"

Through the constant battle to enter a field so filled with men, during a time in history when women's rights were severely limited compared to what they are now, Ruth Bader Ginsburg endured. And on top of that, she excelled and made a habit of challenging the system to ensure that future generations wouldn't experience the same adversities that she did, whether it be on the basis of gender, race, sexual orientation, or any other human right. Throughout her entire career as an attorney, Ginsburg carefully and precisely chipped away at the many gender-discriminatory laws in the United States, which were harmful to all. She then spent nearly three decades as a Supreme Court justice, earning a reputation as a dissenter by steadfastly standing up for equality and human rights.

Ruth Bader Ginsburg faced massive challenges to enter a field so biased against her gender and, as such, flagrantly outside of her expected position in society. Instead of buckling beneath these adversities, she used them as stepping-stones to change the rules of the game so that future generations wouldn't have to struggle as much as she did for equality.

Disruptors Dinner Party

Imagine hosting a dinner party (or brunch if that's more your thing) with any five dreamers turned disruptors of your choosing, dead or alive. Who would you choose for your party, and why? (These can be friends and family, historical figures, politicians, athletes, musicians, researchers . . . whoever you'd like!) In the space below, list the people you'd want to invite, and think about at least one question you'd want to ask each of them. Bonus points if they're somehow related to your own dream!

1. _____

2. _____

3. _____

4. _____

5. _____

Disrupting—It's Not Just in the History Books!

In the section above, you read about why dreamers are predisposed to become disruptors through the examples of a couple of historic disruptors. But disrupting isn't something that only happened in the past, and that we can read about in history books—disrupting is happening *right now*, and by people in our generation! Here are a few young people you may have heard of, who are dreamers just like you, and who have become major disruptors in the world:

- **Greta Thunberg:** *A Swedish environmental activist who has gained international recognition for her straightforward approach while urging world leaders to take* *immediate action to address the climate crisis. She first became known for her activism when, at the age of fifteen, she began spending school days picketing her parliament to address climate change more aggressively.*

- **Aisha Mustafa:** *At the age of nineteen, this physicist invented a space propulsion system that eliminates the need for fuel and thrusters. Her work is based on quantum theory and could ultimately make space travel lighter, cheaper, and more accessible.*

- **Nadya Okamoto:** *As a sixteen-year-old, Nadya cofounded Period.org, a nonprofit aimed at educating the public about menstruation, removing its stigma, and providing period materials for those in need.*

Once you start looking for disruptors, you'll find many young people today who are changing the world, some in big ways (like the three examples above!) and some in much smaller and more local ways.

Recognize Disruptors Close to Home

While all of the disruptors we've discussed here so far are well-known, publicity and magnitude are not what define a disruptor. To be a disruptor, you don't need to be popular on social media, have articles written or videos published about you, or make change at a national or worldwide scale. Being a disruptor means that you're changing the world around you through your passion for your dream, your tenacity in chasing after your dream, and your creativity in how you achieve your dream. You can be a disruptor at a smaller scale simply by affecting those in your close communities, whether that means your school or class, your team or troupe, your group of friends, or even just one other person who is moved by your passion for your dream. Leaving an indelible mark on even one person is enough to make you a disruptor.

I want you to take a minute to think about what that actually means. Think about ways that your specific dream, and the actions that you take to reach it, may end up disrupting those around you. For example, if you were practicing to try out for the varsity soccer team, you may inspire younger kids to give soccer a try as well. That's disrupting! Or perhaps you love hiking and often pick up trash when you're out on a trail—not only does that make the world a cleaner place, but doing so may also prompt the people who see you in action (your friends and family, or even strangers from afar) to litter less, pick up trash that they see, or even recycle properly. Boom, you're a disruptor! Or maybe your disruptive action is something that you hadn't even noticed anyone else was aware of—what if your singing in the shower inspires your mom or dad to join a community choir they've secretly always wanted to be a part of? That's disruption too! As these examples show, disrupting is not always (or even usually) intentional, and it definitely doesn't have to be massive to

have an important impact. Any of these situations—as well as innumerable more that you are likely to encounter on your path to your dream—have the capacity to turn you from dreamer to disruptor.

The ways that your dream might affect the world—starting with, but not limited to, your community—are truly endless! They might mirror the examples above, they might be completely different, and most of all, they might be completely unpredictable to you right now. Don't worry too much about trying to have (or not have) an impact, and instead focus on your dream. Know that doing so will open up opportunities for you to impact others in the future!

People like the Wright brothers, RBG, Bill Gates, or Nadya Okamoto are one in a million. It is the very rare person who is not only able to dream big and be strongly passionate in chasing their dreams, but who is also lucky enough to be alive at the right time and exposed to the right resources. It is such an unpredictable compilation of events that allows any one person to rise to such large and public disruption—which means that it's especially difficult to try to chase down this particular brand of success. And that's why it's important to remember one very simple truth—while large-scale disruptions are often the most talked about, they are by no means the only, nor even the most influential, type of disruption.

Hidden Disruptors Galore

How many disruptors do you know? I bet it's more than you realize. There are people I like to think of as hidden disruptors—those who create disruption without many others recognizing it, often within their own community. Below is a list of types of people who might be disrupting in your community, even if quietly. Can you name one person you know in at least five of these categories who is a "hidden disruptor"? What about them makes you think they're filling that role?

Teachers _____

Neighbors _____

Volunteers _____

Mentors _____

Nurses, Doctors, or Other Medical Professionals _____

_____

Parents _____

Youth Activists _____

Friends _____

Classmates _____

Community Leaders _____

Engineers _____

Scientists _____

School Employees _____

Librarians _____

Youth Leaders _____

Firefighters _____

Coaches _____

Camp Counselors _____

School Club Founders _____

Neighborhood Patrols _____

Politicians _____

Writers or Journalists _____

Caregivers _____

Inventors _____

Artists _____

Business Owners _____

Blood, Organ, or Money Donors _____

_____

The great majority of disruptors aren't recorded in history books or lauded in mass media—the great majority are composed of dreamers and doers who enact change every single day in smaller, quieter ways. Think about it—if there are billions of people on Earth, we don't need each and every one of those people to be mass-scale disruptors. If even a fraction of them are disrupting, changing, and improving their own communities, they are each individually creating a collective massive cultural and social movement. Small actions can and do make a difference in the world as a whole. As modern dreamers, you get to decide what types of actions you want to take and what type of impact you hope to make.

How Do Dreamers Become Disruptors?

Sometimes dreamers become disruptors on purpose. Other times they might stumble into that role accidentally. It can even be some combination of the two! A dreamer becomes a disruptor when their dream starts to positively impact others around them—especially if that impact has a lasting effect over time. You might find that you become a disruptor because the actions you take to accomplish your dream inspire someone else, or because your actions go counter to the way something has previously been done and create a new path. Even if you don't intend to impact anyone else as you chase your dream, you just might do so inadvertently. Oftentimes as we pursue our passions and work to make them a reality, we affect others around us in ways we won't ever even see or know about. While the disruptors we often point to are making sweeping and massive changes, the small ways that pursuing our passions can affect others can be collectively more powerful.

Similarly, disrupting can also happen because achieving your big dream requires you to step out and create your own opportunities in order to make your dream a reality.

There are lots of different, unique ways to become a disruptor—depending on you, your dream, and the community you're engaging with. You might even find that just having a big dream—and talking about it—is disruptive.

Since disruption can happen in so many ways—at different scales and sizes, in different areas of interest, or with different means of making an impact—it can sometimes be difficult to recognize who exactly is a disruptor, especially when they're close to home. Thankfully, there are some telltale features or signs of disruptors that can help you recognize the unique means of disruption happening around you, and even recognize when and how *you* are being (or have already been) a disruptor. These signs may include: having enduring passion for a dream and persisting in pursuing it, being creative in the face of adversity, starting out as the first at something, and being a unique individual. Let's take a look at each of these and think about what they mean—and why they signify disruption.

☑ *Enduring passion and persistence: As we've discussed, sometimes having and chasing after a dream is enough to impact others around you. This is especially true if you're sharing your dream with the world around you—if you're being loud and proud! You might inspire and excite others about whatever the specific topic of your dream is—a love for soccer, for instance, or an interest in cleaner oceans—through talking about your own passion or setting an example by taking actions toward your dream. On* the other hand, your dream might inspire and excite others in a more general way. Rather than recruiting people around you to your particular subject of interest, you might inspire someone to think about and follow their own dreams. Seeing you be brave enough to go after your dreams can influence others to do so as well!

✔️ **Creativity in the face of adversity:** Disruption is about changing the way that things are done or thought about. Often, if something is partly but not entirely broken, people might stick with it and ask: Why change something that's worked well enough so far? Well, things can always be better, and one of the largest driving forces behind any improvement comes into play when someone decides that enough is enough. Being challenged by something forces us to look for different ways to manage that thing better, ways that would never have been even thought of without adversity of some sort. All of which is to say: when searching for disruptors, be sure to look not just at what people are doing, but at why they are doing what they do. You'll likely find that many of them are making big changes because they weren't satisfied with something and were unwilling to accept that things couldn't be better.

✔️ **Being the first:** Whether you're inventing something, pioneering unexplored fields, or taking a stand for social justice, part of being the first person to do something takes a lot of chance and happenstance. You have to luck into being born in the right place and at the right time in history to be the first at something. But the other side of becoming the first person to do something (or even the first person to do something in a particular place or way) is having the will and drive to accomplish it, even when you don't have the example of someone else to work off of or look up to. There always has to be a first person to accomplish something, and doing so will often affect the world for a long time afterward.

(✓) **Being unique:** Ultimately, the one trait that runs through every disruptor—one that will help you recognize disruptors in your own life, or in the world around you—is their uniqueness. Each and every one of us is a unique individual. The way we think, the talents and skills we have, the interests and passions that drive us, and the experiences that shape us are different for every single person. This uniqueness is incredibly powerful, and it holds a lot of potential to change things. Some people embrace this individuality more than others—and doing so is a sign of a disruptor! Those who choose to think differently from others, to act even if they're acting alone or as part of a minority, are the people who introduce new ideas and new technologies, and who lead their communities—and even humanity—forward.

Recognizing Disruptors and Enacting Disruption 🖊

Use these prompts to search out disruptors in your own community—and to become one yourself!

1. In what ways do you see people around you disrupting the status quo? In school? On TV? On social media? What makes their actions disruptive and how are they using these actions for good?

_____

_____

_____

2. How have you been a disruptor—in your school, friend group, family, or elsewhere? Have you enacted disruption either on purpose or unknowingly? To figure out whether you've been a disruptor in your community, ask yourself the following questions: _Have I ever done something even though not many others were interested or involved at the beginning? Have I ever started something? Have I ever faced adversity and persevered? Do I do things differently from other people?_ If you said yes to any of these questions, you're probably already a disruptor!

_____

_____

_____

3. What areas in your own life or surrounding community do you see that need disrupting, and what can you do to start that change? Are there areas that you feel stuck in or that seem like they need a push? Is there anything not working quite as well as you know it could? The first step in disrupting is to identify places or situations that would benefit from being disrupted.

_____

_____

_____

Different Paths to Disruption

Given how many reasons there are for people to become disruptors, I'm sure it won't come as a surprise to hear that disruption can play out in any number of ways. Thinking about those different ways is important for dreamers, because it can help you decide how to go about becoming a disruptor yourself! There are three main categories that I like to sort disruptors into, based on the path that led them to becoming a disruptor. Those categories are: unintentional disruptors, unexpected disruptors, and intentional disruptors.

Unintentional disruptors are dreamers who chase after their dream and just happen to leave a trail of change behind them. In these instances, a person's dream (or the way they go about striving toward it) is so powerful that it winds up changing

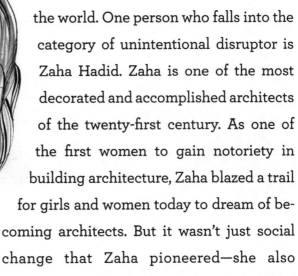

the world. One person who falls into the category of unintentional disruptor is Zaha Hadid. Zaha is one of the most decorated and accomplished architects of the twenty-first century. As one of the first women to gain notoriety in building architecture, Zaha blazed a trail for girls and women today to dream of becoming architects. But it wasn't just social change that Zaha pioneered—she also changed the entirety of what people believed was possible and desired in architecture. Zaha strove to give her buildings features that imitated life, connecting the human experience to the lifeless buildings that shelter us. She left behind a legacy that continues to influence architecture and society today. Much like Zaha, you (as a dedicated dreamer) might burn so bright as you strive toward your dream that you leave a lasting impact on the world even after you've accomplished what you set out to do.

Unexpected disruptors are people who did not initially set out to make a change, but found themselves in a position to do so and actively decided to seize that opportunity. Youth activist Emma González, who survived a mass school shooting and then went on to become the face and voice for a movement for gun control, is one such disruptor. After her school's horrendous and tragic shooting, Emma and her classmates were the focus of national media attention. Alongside some of her peers, Emma grabbed hold of this media spotlight to direct the conversation to what she thought was most important—ensuring that future students wouldn't have to experience what she and her classmates went through. Emma was able to rally young people around the country to participate in school walkouts and other forms of protest to make their voices heard as a collective. She didn't set out to be a gun control activist, but was plunged into this role by a very specific and unique set of circumstances.

At some point or another, you too might realize that, due to unexpected circumstances, you have the ability to use your voice to promote change. It might not be at such a massive scale as Emma, or for as dramatically emotional of a reason, but if you do find yourself in such a position, you will have the chance to make waves.

The last and most direct path toward becoming a disruptor is by engaging in intentional disruption. Intentional disruptors are people who set out with the intent to create change and shake things up. A prime example of this type of disruptor is Elaine Welteroth, the past editor in chief of *Teen Vogue*. Elaine revolutionized *Teen Vogue* by moving the magazine away from a focus on fashion and beauty, and instead shifting it to a focus on topics that have the potential to create deeper change for the readers of the magazine. She used her position to highlight things like intersectional feminism, representation of diversity, politics, and current social justice issues. Notably, these changes didn't just coincidentally occur while Elaine was editor in chief of *Teen Vogue*; they were her intentional next move in a career in which she'd regularly worked to incorporate more diverse views into pop culture. Elaine chased after something that she was passionate about, with the intention of making a lasting difference. If you identify with her story and feel that you'd like to push for your dream to disrupt, then you might be an intentional disruptor just like her!

At the end of the day, dreaming and disrupting go hand in hand. What it really comes down to is, as you go about chasing after your dreams—big or small, personal or public—be aware that you have the ability to make the world a better place, just by virtue of being a dreamer and a doer. Know that your actions, your choices, and even just your thoughts are powerful and can have an impact that you might not be able to imagine yet. You, as a dreamer, might someday become a disruptor. If the examples of past and present dreamers turned disruptors in this chapter have shown us anything, it's that dreams are incredible, but it's the people behind the dreams who truly change the world. And that group of people includes you.

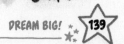

CHAPTER 5

Facing Your Fears

To be brave you must first be afraid. Being brave isn't about not feeling scared. Real courage is all about overcoming your fears.

—Bear Grylls, professional adventurer

When I tell people that I want to become an astronaut, there's a standard set of comments and questions that generally follows. Responses might include anything from surprise and shock at me having such a big dream, to questions about how exactly one becomes an astronaut, to a couple of overused jokes about space cadets. But the one response that pretty much never fails to crop up? That would be people's questions about fear. Time and time again I've been asked questions like: *Are you afraid of space? Of sitting on top of a rocket made out of essentially the same materials as a bomb? Of dying in space and*

never seeing your family or Earth again? Are you afraid of telling
people about this dream and then failing to accomplish it?

People tend to ask these questions for a very good reason. Space—and by extension, human space travel—*is* scary. It's at the top of the list of the most inhospitable places imaginable for humans. Outer space oscillates between being a frozen tundra and a boiling expanse, often over periods of just a couple hours. There's no oxygen, no water, and no food to be found. Spring a leak in your spaceship or space suit and you risk suffocating in the vacuum of space. You're constantly surrounded by radiation, some of which is completely unpredictable in direction and frequency. And all of that's just after you've actually reached space—getting to and from space has its own complex layers of danger (in fact, over the last five decades of human space travel, almost all astronaut deaths have occurred during takeoff and reentry).

Physical safety and well-being aside, becoming an astronaut is an extremely competitive aspiration—the chances of actually accomplishing it are very, very small, and therefore, the chances of failing to reach outer space are quite large. Suffice it to say, fear at the prospect of becoming an astronaut is a normal part of having this dream.

But here's a secret—having a dream is an inherently scary thing, regardless of what that dream is. Becoming an astronaut is a rather extreme example of the fear involved in dreaming, but whether or not a dream involves actual physical danger, every dream invokes fear of failure, fear of the future, and fear of the unknown.

This might all sound really gloomy, but here are three pieces of good news: First off, you're not alone! So many dreamers and doers before you have faced these same fears and come out all right on the other side (and likewise, every dreamer after you will face the same types of fears as you do). Secondly, having fears and doubts doesn't have to stop you from chasing after (and achieving) your dreams—as long as you know how to manage those fears. And lastly, your fears can actually work to help you achieve your dreams, once you learn how to master them!

It's completely normal for chasing after your dreams to be a scary thing. Fear is one of the most basic and innate parts of human nature. It takes courage to have a dream, to talk about that dream, and ultimately, to act toward that dream! Remember, courage isn't the absence of fear, but rather the ability to act in spite of it. It's the thing that allows you to chase after your dream regardless of any doubts you might have. And it's something you can build by facing your fears and anxieties head-on, sizing them up, and learning how to manage them.

As you set out on the path toward achieving your dreams, there are all sorts of fears you might face. You might be afraid of not accomplishing your dream, of finding yourself in new situations and trying new things, of sharing your dreams and goals with the world, or of the general unknown-ness of the future. This chapter will help you learn to recognize your fears and doubts,

develop skills to control and manage them, and ultimately, help you use your fears to guide your path instead of letting them block it.

❗ UNDERSTANDING FEAR

There's a well-known quote from Sun Tzu's *The Art of War* that says, "Know thy enemy." What this piece of advice means at its core is that the very first step to mastering anything standing in your way—whether it's an actual opponent or the roadblock presented by your fears—is to understand it. As you face your fears, it helps to understand them both in the more general sense (What is fear? Why do humans experience it? What purpose does it serve?) and in the personal sense (What are the specific fears that surround your dream? Why do you fear these things?). Before we get to the specific fears, though, let's start with trying to wrap our minds around fear as a general human experience.

Fear is one of our most basic emotions. If having dreams is part of what makes us human, having fears is the flip side. At its core, fear is important to humanity because it has allowed us to survive—and as such, shaped the path of our evolution. Throughout all of human history, it was the people who feared the right things (and, as a result of that fear, avoided them) who survived long enough to have and raise children—children who would then carry **OH NO!**

on those same fear instincts. This is why you likely have fears that you struggle to articulate, but that somewhere deep down you feel are important. For example, a fear of snakes would have been important to your distant ancestors, who spent a lot more time sharing the same environment as them. They were much more likely to encounter, and perish from, a venomous snake than you are today. And yet, even though you no longer face that same danger from snakes, you still have the instinct to be afraid of them. Fear exists for a reason, and as such, should be listened to and respected. But as the previous example shows, not every fear is equally valuable to us (or to you and your individual circumstances)—so blindly accepting your fears and allowing them to dictate your life probably won't work out so well, and definitely won't help you accomplish your dreams.

There are two main points that I think are important to note when considering fear as a central human experience. First, that fear is a byproduct of thinking about and striving toward the future—it's something that helps humans survive and create a future for themselves. And second, that everyone experiences fear at some point, which (like having dreams!) makes it something that ties us all together. All of which is to say that, as much as we may dislike or even dread fear, there's something comforting about knowing that none of us are alone in experiencing it. And since fear is connected to anticipating the future, it's very normal and expected to experience fears and doubts when you start thinking about your future more.

Everyone reacts differently to the emotions and feelings they have surrounding the future. While everyone experiences fear, not everyone is equipped to deal with it—and that makes a big difference. If you don't think about fear and how to handle it before it actually occurs, you likely won't be entirely prepared when you actually encounter it, and it could become an insurmountable roadblock on the path toward your dream. But defining your fears now, and learning how to handle them, will undoubtedly help you as you continue on your way. How do you actually go about recognizing and managing your fears, though? Let's dive in!

MANAGING FEAR ⚡

I'll say it again because it's so important: fear is normal, happens to everyone, and is an inescapable part of having and chasing a dream. We can't avoid experiencing fear, but what we can do is make sure that our fears don't hold us back from our dreams. To do that successfully, it helps to have a two-pronged approach, incorporating both inward-focused self-reflection and outward-focused action.

Self-reflection is great for helping us discover and understand our fears. It makes sense, doesn't it, that to combat our fears we have to first recognize what exactly it is we're afraid of, determine why we're afraid of those particular things, and ultimately choose to value the benefits of facing our fears.

Managing fear by taking action is equally helpful, though! Just knowing what it is you're afraid of (and why!) oftentimes won't be enough for you to fully mitigate the negative effects of that fear—instead, you need to take actions to prepare for and overcome your fears.

Read on for more on how to combine self-reflection and action to not only face and overcome your fears, but also turn your fears into a positive force that will help drive you to accomplish your dream. I know that might seem counterintuitive, but believe me, it works!

DISCOVER YOUR FEARS BEFORE THEY DISCOVER YOU

Just like the first step to chasing your dreams is to figure out what your dream is, the first step to managing your fears is to figure out what it is that you're afraid of—and why! Why? Well, thinking about what your fears are before you actually encounter them will allow you to be much more prepared when you do.

This might be easier for some people than others—and it might be easier to pinpoint certain fears over others as well! In fact, you might have a fear that you're already aware of, and you might even already recognize how it affects your dream. I had that happen to me when I was a kid, because I knew full well about one fear that I had: I was deathly afraid of needles. This is a big problem for someone aspiring to become an astronaut since astronauts are essentially the guinea pigs of space travel: to learn more about the effects of space travel on humans, astronauts have to submit to all kinds of health examinations and experiments before, during, and after their time in space. It's very likely that those examinations and experiments will include things like taking blood samples or administering medicines intravenously, all of which boils down to needles being a not infrequent occurrence for space travelers. I knew about this fear of mine early on, because needles are something I'd already encountered by way of flu shots and other necessary immunizations, and was able to connect it to my dream after reading accounts of what it was like to travel to space from past astronauts.

Define Your Fears

Are there any fears that you already know you have? Think about anything that you're afraid of that could affect your ability to chase after your dream. In the space on the next page, write down three things that you find frightening. Once you've written them down, reread your list and ask yourself, *Are any of these fears connected to my dream? How?*

I'm frightened by . . .

1. _____

2. _____

3. _____

Knowing some of your fears ahead of time is great, and can definitely help you on your way to overcoming them. But of course, not all fears are quite so easy to get a handle on—either because you haven't encountered them yet and therefore can't possibly know to be afraid of them, or because some fears are simply more elusive and difficult to pinpoint than others. This second possibility might be the case if your fear is of something that's not physical: recognizing that you're afraid of something tangible (like heights or swimming) is much easier than realizing that you're afraid of something abstract (such as failure, rejection, or change).

Discovering Abstract Fears

Use the following guided journaling exercise to evaluate your dream and search out any abstract fears that might hold you back from achieving it.

Circle your answer (or fill in your own word in the blank space!) for the following:

* When I think about my dream, I feel . . . **anxious / nervous / scared /_____ / none of these things.**
* When I think about the actions I'll take to reach my dream (your plan from chapter 3!), I feel . . . **anxious / nervous / scared / _____ / none of these things.**

I procrastinate on my dream and don't know why: **yes / no.**

If you answered any of the questions above in a way that made you think you might have some fears that you're not completely aware of (maybe your dream makes you anxious, for example, but you're not sure why, or perhaps one of the steps in your plan is scaring you for reasons that seem unclear to you), take a look at the following list of common fears that can hold people back from their dreams. Circle a number to indicate how much you think each fear applies to you (with 0 being not at all, 5 being completely). Then think about how these might be connected to your dream or plan.

Change	0	1	2	3	4	5
Failure	0	1	2	3	4	5
Being judged	0	1	2	3	4	5
Getting hurt	0	1	2	3	4	5
The unknown	0	1	2	3	4	5

CHOOSE TO FACE YOUR FEARS !

It may take you some time to discover your fears, and new ones might even crop up as you continue down the path toward your dream—and that's okay! There are some fears you really won't know about until you start down the path toward your dream. For example, if you want to become a soccer goalie, it might take trying to play a game or two to realize that you're afraid of objects flying at you! Whenever you do encounter fears, though, it's up to you to make the deliberate choice to face them. Facing and overcoming your fears can be difficult, and to do it successfully, you'll need plenty of self-motivation and dedication. So the more actively you choose to work past them, the more likely you are to conjure up the necessary drive and courage to face your fears head-on. Choosing to face your fears instead of waiting for them to block your path allows you to set yourself up for

success—you get to handle them at your own pace, in a more controlled way, and with as much preparation as possible. Making the choice to face your fears on your terms means that you get to step outside your comfort zone not because you're forced to, but because you've chosen to. And by doing so, you'll be better able to grow past your fears.

Bear Grylls is one of the most qualified people to talk about choosing to face your fears head-on—both in your broader life and while chasing after your dream! Bear was a serviceperson in the British Army's special forces unit, and has since become a survival instructor, a television personality in numerous wilderness survival shows, a public speaker, an author, and an explorer of such remote and extreme environments as Antarctica, Mount Everest, and others! Truly, anything that strikes fear into people's hearts, Bear Grylls has probably already done. He had his fair share of wild adventures and experiences, but there's one in particular that almost cost Bear his life—and that has since inspired him to tackle his fears head-on at every opportunity. When he was twenty-one years old, Bear broke his back in three places during a skydiving accident, when his parachute failed to deploy properly. He ended up spending a year in rehab, and he wasn't sure he would ever even walk again. Just eighteen months after the accident, though, Bear not only walked but achieved what had been a lifelong dream of his: to become the youngest British person in history to summit the tallest mountain on Earth—Mount Everest. Since then, Bear has chosen not to let fear stand in his way, no matter what! Just like Bear, you too can overcome your fears, and achieve your dream, by *choosing* to face your fears head-on.

List Your Motivations!

Consider why you want to overcome your fears—how will doing so help you reach your dream? Use the following space to keep track of all your great reasons! Write out a list of the benefits of overcoming your fears. Keep it to reflect back on when you face those fears and are feeling challenged by them.

_____

_____

_____

_____

_____

_____

TAKE ACTION TO FACE YOUR FEARS

Sometimes figuring out what it is that you're afraid of—and why—is enough to help you get over those fears and keep them from affecting your ability to chase after your dream. The human brain is amazing—just recognizing what your emotions are and why you're feeling them can help you control them. But most of us will face some type of fear that we can't quite shake (I know I have!) no matter how self-aware we are. In these instances it's good to have other tools that you can count on to help you overcome your fears. And the good news is that there is a wide variety of skills you can develop and utilize to take action in facing your fears. Remember that everyone is different and unique, and the ways that we can successfully manage our fears are just as different and unique. Feel free to choose to use one, a couple, or any other combination of the skills on the next page—whatever works for you!

CONSIDER THE "WORST-CASE SCENARIO"

The truth of the matter is that regardless of what we do, at some point in our lives it's likely that we're going to fail at things, and that includes failing at overcoming our fears. You could do everything "right" whenever possible as you chase your dreams, and you might still end up failing at something along the way. Life is unpredictable, and many things in it are out of our control. Failure is sometimes inevitable—and in many cases, it can even turn out to be a good thing! We'll talk about anticipating and using failure to your advantage a lot more in the next chapter, but for now the important thing to keep in mind is that sometimes you might end up in a situation where your fears come true.

A great way to try to overcome your fears is to honestly consider the worst thing that could happen if your fear were to come true—in other words, your worst-case scenario. While it might seem counterproductive to think about the most negative possibility, doing so can actually provide a pathway to feeling less anxiety and stress about your fears. Oftentimes when you think logically about your fears, you'll find that the worst thing that could happen is not really as bad as you'd been imagining it before. Our brains like to trick us into making mountains out of molehills—when we don't keep our imaginations in check, our minds can conjure up a worst-case scenario that's way worse than anything that could ever really hap-pen. Use the following guided journaling to ensure that you're keeping your fears properly sized and not letting them get bigger than they need to be!

What's the Worst That Could Happen?

Choose just one of the fears that you identified earlier in this chapter to consider here. Answer the following questions based on that fear.

★ Define your worst-case scenario by asking yourself: *What is truly the worst thing that could happen if this fear were to come true?*

_____

_____

* If this worst-case scenario were to occur, what would the effect be?

  _____

  _____

* How likely is this worst-case scenario to occur? _____

  _____

* If your worst-case scenario were to occur, what could you do to handle it? What actions could you take to mitigate it and ensure that the effect is minimal? Write down three ideas or steps of how you would handle your own personal worst-case scenario.

  _____

  _____

TURN YOUR FEAR INTO EXCITEMENT!

Rather than searching for calmness in the face of fear, consider embracing the heightened emotions that come along with it. Turning your fear into excitement is one of the fastest and most effective ways to fuel your dreams. Let's think about why this works.

One of the most important ideas to remember is that, when you feel fear, you don't just experience it by way of intangible thoughts and emotions. You do have those, but in addition, your body reacts with physiological changes, including things like an elevated heart rate, fast and shallow breathing, or even an adrenaline rush. These responses are related to a concept you may have heard of called the fight-or-flight response. Essentially, your fear triggers your body to either run away from or stand up to the thing causing you fear, and it provides you with the physical tools to help you do one or the other. But when you think about it, these responses that your body offers up are pretty similar to the physical responses you experience when you're excited about something! Because of this, it's much easier to transfer your fear into excitement than it is to do a full about-face and completely switch to a calm state of mind.

The very first step in shifting fear to excitement is recognizing when you're feeling afraid. When you start to feel anxious, nervous, or afraid of something, take a couple deep breaths and a moment to analyze your thoughts. Shifting fear to excitement is all about catching your fears early on and changing the way you're thinking about the thing causing you fear. For example, if you're afraid or anxious about your first day of basketball practice, dance class, or anything else that you're trying for the first time, you might be having thoughts along the lines of: *What if I'm not good at this thing?*, *What if I embarrass myself in front of my peers?*, or *What if I mess up?* It's very normal to feel negative thoughts when you're experiencing fear. But if you realize that you're thinking these things because of the fear itself, and not necessarily because they're true or logical, you can try to change them! In this instance you might try to offer yourself responses to your internal questions such as: *The fact that I'm new means I have a lot of potential to improve!*, *Everyone is going to be new—nobody will be judging me!*, and *I'm doing this thing because I'm interested in it—I'm going to have fun!* The key to this shift is to make sure that the new thoughts that you're introducing feel true to you. Next time you find yourself in a fearful moment, try shifting your fear into excitement!

CULTIVATE A GROWTH MINDSET!

Much like shifting your fear into excitement, this next skill for managing your fears requires a conscious and intentional shift of thought. Cultivating a growth mindset is a great tool to use, and it can help you feel more comfortable and less wary of chasing your dreams and overcoming your fears. *But wait,* I can almost hear you asking, *what even is a "growth mindset"?* Great question.

The basic theory here is that people can have a "fixed mindset," where they believe that their abilities, talents, and potential are all set in stone and unchangeable, or a "growth mindset," where they believe that they can change these things—and improve them—over time. The byproduct of each mindset is then fairly obvious, right? A fixed mindset removes your personal agency, taking away your ability to work hard and work smart toward improving, while a growth mindset enables you to hold on to those very things. Let's look at an example of how this might affect a dream!

Say you want to learn another language. When you first start out, you might struggle with certain aspects of it, such as new rules for spelling, sounds that you're not used to using, different grammar patterns, new vocabulary to memorize, and more! If you have a fixed mindset, you'd believe that you're not capable of learning new skills or changing how you think—what's hard at the beginning will stay hard as you continue to learn more of the language. However, if you have a growth mindset, you'd recognize that these things are all skills that you can improve on, even if you're not very good at them to start off with!

Most of us have some combination of fixed and growth mindsets already. The exciting thing is that you can increase the amount of time you spend building a growth mindset! Doing this involves two main things: self-reflection and practice. Many of the self-reflection activities throughout this book can help you develop the skills to look inward and analyze your thoughts, ideas, and abilities. As you do them, keep in mind that you always have room for improvement—and then act accordingly! Cultivating a growth mindset is all about increasing the quantity *and* quality of time you spend practicing your chosen skill—essentially, to improve at something you have to not only spend more time on it but also make sure that time is focused. Put in the time and effort to improve, and know that the results can surprise you!

PRACTICE VISUALIZING YOUR FEARS!

In addition to cultivating a growth mindset and practicing consistently, another way to work on overcoming your fears is through visualization. Visualization is when you think of or imagine something before it's actually happened, and it can be a

powerful tool. Successful people in all fields use visualization to improve their skills and prepare themselves for success. It's very common among professionals ranging from athletes to musicians and even pilots! In fact, it's so common for pilots to learn through visualization that there's something called "chair flying," when a pilot sits down anywhere that isn't actually in an airplane, closes their eyes, and then imagines the cockpit. The pilot then goes through the various steps of takeoff, landing, emergency procedures, and more—all in their imaginary airplane.

I myself am a pilot, and this "chair flying" method actually saved my life once. That might sound like an exaggeration, but it's true! When I was training to be a pilot I spent a lot of time thinking about all the things that could go wrong in the air—engine fires, radio failures, stalls, and more. Having the responsibility for not just my own life but also the lives of my passengers made me afraid in a way I'd never been afraid before. But I couldn't fly if I allowed that fear to control me. Practice, through visualization or "chair flying," was the solution that let me instead be in control of—and actually benefit from—my fear. I found that thinking about all of these worst-case scenarios, and then practicing the solutions to them through visualization, made me a more confident and courageous pilot. In-flight emergencies (like most worst-case scenarios) are rare—but they do happen. By "chair flying," I knew that when (not *if*) an emergency happened while I was in the pilot seat, I'd be able to handle it because I'd already thought through my options, chosen a course of action, and developed muscle memory so that I could react immediately. Essentially, I'd already handled each emergency dozens of times before and been successful at doing so.

This philosophy of preparing for both success and failure served me well when, during a practice flight before my final examinations, I was demonstrating how to recover from a stall and ended up in a spin. A stall is a situation in which too little air flows over the wings of the plane to continue creating the lift needed to hold the plane in the air. As you can imagine, not enough lift leads to an airplane losing altitude instead of gaining it! That was bad enough on its own, but the spin, which is when a plane spins uncontrollably around one wing and loses altitude, made it even worse. Not only did the plane drop like a rock, but a spin is very disorienting to the pilot—imagine being on a carnival ride where up and down get flipped every second! When my plane spun while I was piloting it, though, I was able to react correctly immediately, because I knew instinctively (after having practiced so much) that recovering from a spin required a specific set of adjustments. I was able to change the power settings, ailerons, rudders, and elevators within seconds, and by doing so, stop the plane from spinning and return to smooth flight.

Now, most situations that you're afraid of won't truly be life or death like my airplane spin experience was, but I guarantee that practicing your reactions to fear through visualization will help you to feel confident in your ability to face—and overcome—that fearful moment. While it's common for people to want to visualize the final result of all their work (winning a gold medal or earning a standing ovation sounds pretty nice to imagine, doesn't it?), it's actually more important—and more helpful!—to spend time visualizing the steps you'll need to take to achieve that final result. This is especially true if you're using visualization as a tool to manage and overcome fear. Exposing yourself to your fears in your mind through visualization can help desensitize you to those fears, ensuring that you don't panic when you encounter them, and are instead able to implement the correct actions to ensure a successful outcome.

To create your own visualization of overcoming your fears, start by finding a quiet place where you can focus and relax. Close your eyes and imagine yourself in your fear-based situation. Try to incorporate as many sensory experiences as you can to convince your brain that the visualization is real. For example, if I were to visualize my fear of heights, I might imagine myself walking up to the top of a tall tower and would incorporate the sound of the wind at the top of the tower, the feeling of the gusts rushing over me, and the gnawing sensation that heights give me in the pit of my stomach. You might be totally cool with heights but have a different fear, such as a fear of being in large crowds, or of sudden, loud noises. In those cases you visualizing your fear might include imagining the feeling of lots of people standing close around you, the sound of a whole mass of voices talking at the same time, the sense of tightness that leaves in your stomach; or you might visualize an abrupt crash of thunder and the way it makes your nerves feel jittery.

Visualization is a skill, and as such you shouldn't expect to be perfect at it right away! It will probably take some practice to visualize the situation as you'd like it to be and to guide yourself through your possible actions. Every time that you work on

visualization, try to go through a couple different scenarios of how facing your fears could go, until you find what you think will be your most successful set of actions.

Visualize Your Fear Through Art

Use the empty comic strip below to think about and draw out the steps that you'd like to incorporate into your visualizations to overcome your fear. It doesn't matter if you think of yourself as a good artist or not—it's perfectly fine to use stick figures for this comic strip! The point isn't to create a masterpiece, but rather to think through the steps you could take to overcome one of your fears.

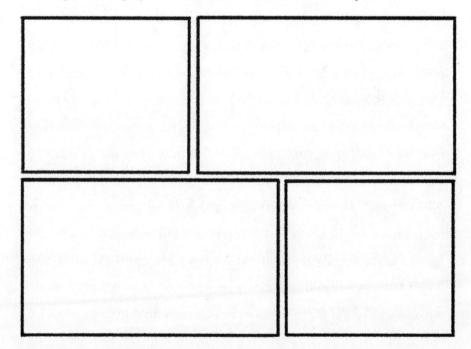

Turn Fear into a Social Experience!

Here's one of the worst things about fear: it can feel very isolating. I'm sure it won't shock you to hear that, because chances are most of you have at some point not only felt afraid, but also felt like no one else truly understood your fear. I know I've had that happen to me. Happily, though, even if that sense of loneliness is your immediate reaction to certain fears, it doesn't have to play out that way. All you need to do is take your fears and make them social!

There are two ways that you can turn your fears into a social experience so that you don't have to feel alone: by finding someone to talk to about them, and by learning about other people who have faced and overcome fear before you. Talking to someone about your fears can be incredibly helpful in managing your level of fear, gaining the confidence to face your fears, and generally seeking out advice on how to overcome them. It might seem scary at first to share your fears with someone else—fear can be a very personal thing. But I guarantee that talking to someone about your fears will be helpful.

If you think that you'd like to talk to someone about your fears, start by thinking about the people in your life who you'd be comfortable talking to about such a personal topic. Just like when you were thinking about who you could share your dreams with, it's possible that you have multiple people in your life who fit the bill. These people might be family members, teachers, religious advisors, coaches, a therapist, or anyone else you'd like! Because pretty much everyone has faced fear at some point, many people will be happy to help you manage your own fears by listening to you and, if you'd like, offering advice. However, unless you reach out and tell these people that you're experiencing fear and would like some help, they likely won't know, and therefore can't help you! All you have to do is ask.

As you go about chasing after your dreams and facing down your fears, one of the most important things to remember is that, even though it might sometimes feel that way, *you are not alone.* You are not the first person to feel the things that you're probably feeling at this point. Worry, anxiety, trepidation—all the emotions that come along with fear are emotions that countless people have experienced before. Not only are you not the first person to feel fear, you're part of the majority!

Learning about the fears that some of the super-successful dreamers who came before you had, and how they overcame them, can help you to not feel isolated. For example, did you know that the historical leaders Abraham Lincoln and Mahatma Gandhi and famous actors Harrison Ford and Julia Roberts all shared a common fear of public speaking? Wild, right? of these people are known around the world for their public speaking and performing, and yet they each started out with serious fear of speaking in front of others. Each of them used specific tools and techniques to ultimately overcome their fear—and the great thing is, we can read up on them and borrow their techniques! So if you have a dream of being in your school play but are worried about getting up in front of a crowd, you can look to people like these as models. And this doesn't just go for public speaking—I guarantee you that whatever your fear is, someone else has felt it (and overcome it) before you. And in this day and age of the internet, finding out about other people's successes in overcoming their fears is easier than ever!

Learn from Others' Fears!

Make a list of five people who have overcome their fears and who inspire you to do the same. How did they manage their fears? What

motivated them to do so? You can include people you've read about in this book, people in your own life, celebrities, historical figures, or anyone else that you'd like!

1. _____

2. _____

3. _____

4. _____

5. _____

I'll say it one more time: Everyone feels fear at some point in time. It's natural and normal. But that doesn't mean that you have to let fear stand in the way of you achieving your dreams. Thinking about your fears in a positive and proactive light gives you the ability to manage them and their effect on you. Most importantly, thinking about your specific fears and how they affect your ability to reach your dream allows you to learn and practice skills to deal with them. The more aware you are of your fears, and your ability to handle those fears, the more likely you are to be successful at achieving your dreams in the long run. Give yourself the opportunity to be your most courageous and confident you by embracing your fears today!

CHAPTER 6

Failure to Launch

If everything was perfect, you would never learn and you would never grow.

—Beyoncé, world-famous entertainer

In the last chapter, we talked a lot about planning for, encountering, and overcoming your fears (and in some instances, planning to avoid these fears altogether). And everything that was said in that chapter remains true! But sometimes, despite all of our best efforts, fears can get the better of us. And when we think about that, there's one really obvious question that comes to mind: What if some of our fears—and especially the fear of failure—come true? What do we do then? Because let's face it— no matter how hard we try, how much we plan ahead, or how strong our dreams are, the fact of the matter is that failure is sometimes inevitable.

Hold on now! Before you start to fully panic, let me clarify what I mean here. I'm not saying that failure is inevitable in the long run—of course not! I fully believe in you and your ability to achieve your dream. But at the same time, I have no doubt that you will likely face failure along the way. How do I know this? Because pretty much every single dreamer before you (myself included!) has failed at some point or another. The history of chasing after dreams is absolutely filled to the brim with failure and mistakes. Life in general is full of failures and mistakes, so there's really no way to completely avoid them.

The good news is that in most cases we come out just fine on the other side. In fact, in many instances facing failures and experiencing mistakes actually allows us to become stronger, more focused, and more determined than we were before the failure or mistake. Failure really can be a good thing for dreamers—it all depends on how you view failure before it happens and how you respond to it once it does. If you expect to fail along the path to your dream and have the tools and skills necessary to manage that failure, you'll find that your failures can become stepping-stones to success instead of insurmountable roadblocks. I can say with great confidence that you will likely fail as you reach for your dream—and I can also assure you that this failure will actually help you achieve it! I've been chasing my big dream of becoming an astronaut and someday walking on the surface of Mars for a *long* time now, and along the way I've run into many failures, and made many mistakes, big and small.

The first really BIG failure that I remember experiencing occurred when I was sixteen years old. I was in my first semester at the University of Minnesota and was taking my first-ever college classes, including a slightly more advanced chemistry class that I had placed into. I faced one immediate problem, though . . . I had *never* actually taken a chemistry class before! I just happened to have placed into the advanced chem class because I had a good foundation in other sciences and because, well, I was good at taking tests. Even knowing that I didn't have a good basis in chemistry and that I had barely scored high enough to enter the advanced class, I chose to challenge myself by taking it. This ended up being a mistake—but in the long run, it was a really good mistake.

Since I didn't have the proper background (or really any background) in chemistry, I of course found myself struggling with the material. On top of that, though, I also struggled with the structure of the class. In high school, which was what I was used to, I'd had about forty fellow students in my classes; this chemistry class, on the other hand, had roughly five hundred students in it! Because of this massive size, it was a much more hands-off class—and as someone who learns through discussion and practice, this was not good news for me. When the semester ended, I wound up with a C-, and I was absolutely devastated.

(Okay, a C- might not seem like a big deal, but up until that point I had consistently been a straight-A student, so to me it felt like a massive failure!) I remember going home after getting my end-of-semester grades and running into my mom's arms to cry my eyes out. I felt like, if I had already failed during my very first semester of college, maybe I wouldn't be able to succeed at all—maybe I just wasn't cut out for academia. Even worse, I worried, what if I wasn't smart enough to be a scientist? How was I going to ever become an astronaut if I couldn't even pass a college chemistry class?? I truly felt like this was the end of my dream.

Luckily for me, my mom didn't share my concerns. Once I stopped crying and explained to her why I was so distraught, she looked at me and said: "So, how are you going to fix this? What can you do to make it better?" She assured me that this failure wasn't a reflection on my ability or intelligence, that I could still accomplish my big dream, and that I could get past this. And it turned out, she was right! I was able to retake the class the next semester and have the C- erased from my transcript and replaced by a new grade. The next semester, when I took the class again, I learned from my previous failure—I changed the way I studied, I found a tutor to help me understand the material better, and in the end I received an A.

When I was sixteen years old and experiencing this failure, it felt like the worst thing ever—it honestly felt like the end of my dream. But when I look back with all the hindsight that I now have, I'm actually incredibly thankful that it happened. Failing at that chemistry class forced me to think critically about how I learned and studied. I learned how to work harder and smarter—skills that allowed me to crush it in my future classes. I also learned how to manage failure—which was important because I had many more failures yet to come! I was really fortunate that, through all of this, I had my mom to help guide me and make it all into a learning experience. Now I want to share the skills I learned with you so that when you face failure on the way to your dream, you're ready to take it in stride and keep on going. In this chapter, you'll learn to anticipate failure before it happens, change your mindset to find triumph in your failures and mistakes, learn and grow from your failures, and most importantly, never stop giving it another try. Does all that sound good and useful? Let's dig in!

EXPECT FAILURE !

The very first, and most important, thing that I can tell you about anticipating failure is that you should *expect to fail*. I know I've already said it, but it bears repeating: you will almost definitely fail at some point. Making mistakes and experiencing failure are inescapable parts of life, possibly even more so when you're working toward a dream. If you deny that failure happens (and that it will eventually happen to *you*), then you won't be ready to manage it and grow from that failure when it comes your way!

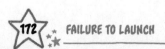

And that really would not be much fun. I want you to think about facing failure early on so that you know how to use it to your advantage.

But wait . . . what really is failure, and what does it look like? Well, that's a hard question to answer because failures come in all different shapes and sizes depending on you, your circumstances, and what you're trying to do. Failure might mean messing up at something, not accomplishing a goal, or otherwise not meeting your own expectations. While failure is different for each and every one of us, here are a couple of examples you might have already encountered: getting a low grade on a test or

quiz at school, messing up your lines in the school play, missing a goal in a sports game, forgetting to keep a promise, or even not meeting your own goals of how often you'd like to practice at or work on something. As you can see, "failure" is really a super-broad term and can apply to lots of different things. And what it all comes down to is that the only person who gets to decide or define what counts as a failure to you is . . . you. Just like how your dreams and goals are yours, what you consider a failure is also completely up to you.

Here's the thing about failure: everyone fails. Think about something you've been passionate about in the past—was it all smooth sailing as you got started? Probably not! You've probably failed at something before, because everyone fails before they can find success. For example, the last time you started a new sport, you probably made a lot of mistakes as you learned the rules. Everyone makes mistakes when they're new to something, and oftentimes even when they're not so new. This is important to keep in mind because it means that, when you do fail, *you are not alone*. You're actually in really good company! Every person you consider to be successful—from your personal heroes to global leaders and everyone in between—has failed before they achieved their success. This is a nice thing to think about, because it shows that failing doesn't mean that you're on the wrong path. In fact, it actually implies that you're on the right one! If so many incredibly successful and awesome people failed just like you did (or even more dramatically than you did!),

then it's a lot easier to feel hopeful about your future and your ability to achieve your dream in the face of failure.

Easily one of the most famous singers in the world, **Beyoncé** holds more records than I can count, has performed in some of the most prestigious venues, and is basically a household name around the world. She's become so successful that now when you talk about "the Queen," it's necessary to clarify whether you mean the Queen of England or Beyoncé, whose nickname is Queen Bey. And although she's so famous now that it may seem like she's just always been a walking, talking success, that's definitely not true—Queen Bey went through her fair share of struggles and failures before making it big. When she was just eight years old, Beyoncé experienced one of her first big failures. Beyoncé and three other girls, who together formed a band called Girls Tyme, performed and competed on *Star Search* (at that time the biggest national talent show on TV). Even after going all out for their dream, and putting their dream out there for the world to see, the group lost the competition. Instead of letting this failure stop her, though, Beyoncé continued to dream big and work hard, going on to form the massively popular and successful girl group Destiny's Child (ask your parents, they'll know who they are!) and eventually striking out on her own solo career, which we all know the result of. So, if you experience failure on the road to your dream, don't worry—you're in good company! Just like Beyoncé, by having the right attitude, a good support system to believe in you, and the drive to keep going when the going gets tough, you too can reach your dream!

You Are Not Alone in Failing!

We often have a tendency to look at failure as this terrible, unusual thing. But in reality, failure isn't entirely a bad thing, and it's definitely not infrequent. Some of the most successful people out there failed massively and frequently before achieving their dreams and successes. Here are some examples of successful, well-known people who have failed on their path to success, along with some thoughts they've had on their failures.

You'll notice empty spaces at the end of this list—fill them in with personal heroes of your own! Find and write down what they've said about failure. Look them up online, or, if they're people you know personally, go ahead and ask them for their thoughts directly.

- **Oprah Winfrey:** *"There's no such thing as failure. Failure is just life trying to move us in another direction."*

- **Michael Jordan:** *"I can accept failure, everyone fails at something. But I can't accept not trying."*

- **Theodor Seuss Geisel (aka Dr. Seuss):** *"I'm sorry to say so but, sadly, it's true that bang-ups and hang-ups can happen to you."*

- **Heleen Snelting:** *"I remind myself that not succeeding is fine, not trying is not. You'll surprise yourself, I guarantee."*

- **President Abraham Lincoln:** *"My greatest concern is not whether you have failed, but whether you are content with your failure."*

- **Bill Gates:** *"It's fine to celebrate success but it is more important to heed the lessons of failure."*

_____: " _____

_____ "

_____: " _____

_____ "

_____: " _____

_____ "

Be Your Own Expert at Failure (and Success!)

We've looked at plenty of other people and their thoughts and opinions on success and failure. But the most important authority for you on success and failure is . . . you! Imagine that you've overcome failure and achieved your dream. What would you want others to know about failure? Or better yet, what would you tell yourself about failure? In the space below, write your own inspiring, insightful quote about failure and success.

_____

_____

_____

_____

_____

_____

_____

FAILURE—IT MIGHT BE OUT OF YOUR CONTROL!

Here's another thing about failure: failure is not a reflection on you or your capacity to be awesome and achieve your dream. Sometimes failure is a message that you're just not ready yet—that circumstances just aren't quite lining up right at this moment, or that you don't have the proper skills at this point in time. You might need to work on time management, follow-through, efficient learning, or skills specific to your dream, like the best technique to throw a football, knowing how to read sheet music, or learning a coding language. Instead of seeing failure as a message from the universe telling you that you are not capable of achieving your dreams (or even just accomplishing one task along the way), see it as a message that says, *Not right now, not yet. Try again!* Failing at something doesn't mean that you can't or won't ever be successful at whatever it is you failed at—it just means that you weren't successful the first time. But who knows, maybe you'll be successful the second, third, fourth, or even fifteenth time that you try! That's actually exactly what happened to one of my personal heroes, astronaut Clayton Anderson.

Clayton Anderson is an astronaut who applied to the NASA astronaut corps no fewer than *fifteen times*. He failed the selection fourteen of those times, but then, on his fifteenth try, he was selected to become an astronaut! As a member of the astronaut corps, he filled important roles here on Earth; he provided essential support for multiple missions to space in varying capacities (such as being a member of the backup crew), and he even got to be an aquanaut, during which time he lived in an underwater laboratory for fourteen days! He also, as the title astronaut suggests, actually went to space, where he spent 152 days living and working on the International Space Station. It took Clayton fifteen years from the time he submitted his first application to the time he joined the astronaut corps, and in that period, he applied every time new astronaut selections were held. How's that for perseverance? If Clayton had taken that first rejection from NASA (or even the second, third, or fourteenth rejection) as a sign that he wouldn't succeed in becoming an astronaut, he

never would have ended up in space.

Now, Clayton isn't a hero of mine just because of his perseverance. He also serves as an inspiration because he used each of his failures to guide him toward his dream. Instead of simply submitting the same application time and again in the hopes of wearing NASA down, each year he asked himself, *How can I make my application better next time? How can I improve myself?* And then he acted on this self-reflection. Clayton spent the time in between his rejections doing things like learning to scuba dive, getting a pilot's license, and becoming the manager of the NASA Johnson Space Center's Emergency Operations Center. He learned from every rejection that he faced, never gave up on his dreams, and eventually found himself in space!

Self-Reflect on a Time You've Failed!

Take a moment to channel your inner Astronaut Clayton Anderson. Use the space below to engage in self-reflection about a failure you've experienced, and plan how you can grow from that failure!

★ What is something that you've failed at in the past? (This could be something large or small, something that happened recently or long ago—really, anything!) _____

_____

★ How did you respond to this failure? Did you try again?
Yes / No
If yes: How many times did you try? _____

★ Did you keep trying at it until you succeeded? **Yes / No**
If no: Why didn't you try again? _____

_____

★ In hindsight, are you happy that you didn't try again or are you disappointed? Why or why not? _____

_____

★ List three things that you could do differently or in addition in order to be successful if you were to try the thing you failed at again.

1. _____

2. _____

3. _____

Now let's talk about something that can be hard to stomach: sometimes success and failure are completely out of your control. You might experience failure not because of something you did (or didn't do) but rather because of inescapable factors in your environment. You can try your hardest and do everything right and still end up failing—in fact, you might find that happening more often than you'd expect. Not to worry, though: this is super normal! Here are some tips to keep in your mental toolbox that can help you handle failing at something even though you tried your hardest.

(✓) *First off, take a moment to be proud of yourself! Putting your best foot forward and giving something your all is incredibly admirable. Not getting the results you'd been hoping for doesn't negate the hard work that you did.*

(✓) *Next, ask yourself,* Have I really done everything that I possibly could to succeed at this? *Try really hard to be truthful with yourself when answering this question. Maybe there's something that you could do—something you could learn, prepare for, or improve on—that you hadn't thought of before. There's nothing wrong with not having done everything you could have on the* first attempt, but it definitely helps to be honest with yourself about that if you're hoping to succeed the next time you try.

(✓) *Now think about what external factors prevented you from being successful. Was your timing off? Were you missing some necessary supplies or information? Did something unexpected affect your performance? The only things that we can control are our mindsets and actions—we can't control anyone or anything else! But we can change the way that we interact with other people and things, or plan to avoid them altogether. If you want to remove some external roadblock that caused you to fail, you have to know what that thing was.*

(✓) *And finally, try again! But maybe don't try again right away, or in the same exact way as before. Use the steps above to inform your decision on when and how to try again. If you found that there actually was something more that you could have done to improve your chances of success, take the time to learn or do that thing. If you identified something external that negatively affected you, think about what you could do differently this time to avoid or respond to that external factor.*

I once heard someone say, "Fail often, fail fast," and it's an idea that I think is key in reaching for your dreams. It's important to take the time after a failure to analyze, understand, and learn from it. But it's also important to not spend too long looking back.

Don't let yourself get stuck dwelling on your past failures—once you've spent an appropriate amount of time learning from a failure or mistake, move on! Look forward, to the future, and move on from your failures quickly to ensure they don't end up holding you back from being brave and audacious in the future. Each of us needs to find our own right balance for how long that might take. I can't tell you exactly how long you should spend thinking back on a failure (I wish I could!), because this is a unique experience for each dreamer. What I can do is tell you to keep this in mind: through trial and error, *you* will figure out your own ideal amount of time to reflect over failures and mistakes.

And above all, when you experience failure, remember this: whether or not it was something that you could have controlled or avoided, be proud that you tried. The biggest failure of all is to not even try in the first place, because if you don't, you have a zero percent chance of succeeding. Your odds can't get worse than that, so you might as well try! Be proud that you tried, be thoughtful and honest with yourself about why you failed, and then, when you're ready, give it another shot (or fifteen).

GROW FROM FAILURE

Failure is inescapable—and honestly, we shouldn't try to escape failure. Rather than running away or hiding from failures and mistakes, we should embrace failure as the awesome

opportunity that it is! Failure is an essential part of learning and growing. If we never failed we would never have to try harder, challenge ourselves, change the way we do things, or *grow*.

Truly, failure and success are not polar opposites of one another (even though most of us have been raised to view them that way). Failure and success don't make for an "either-or" situation, nor are they an "all-or-nothing" pair of ideas. Failure is an essential part of success. You can think of failure as a growing pain. It's uncomfortable, distressing at the time, and you'd likely rather not experience it. But I bet you probably like getting taller—and you can't do that without a few growing pains. Similarly, you probably like improving and succeeding, but you can't do those things without also experiencing failures and mistakes.

A way to think about this in more concrete terms is to think about the writing process. It might surprise you to hear that most people—even famous and successful writers—aren't completely happy with something the very first time that they write it. (I know I'm certainly not—and that includes my writing in this very book!) You've probably experienced this as well, whether while writing for fun or writing something for school. It usually takes some time after you've written something to improve it—maybe you read it through a second time and made some edits, maybe you had someone else read it and comment on it, or maybe you've even scrapped an entire piece and started over from scratch! Improvement, and eventual success, only really happens after failures and mistakes. It may not always be the most fun or comfortable experience, but it is a necessary and helpful one. When you weigh out the pros and cons of growing pains vs. not growing at all, the pains are worth it. And when you balance the pros and cons of failure, the pains of failure are definitely worth it in the long run.

So instead of seeing mistakes and failures as personal deficiencies, try instead to see them as opportunities! Experiencing failure and making mistakes gives us a more humble outlook. They guide you to figure out and focus on what you need to do *now* to be more successful at achieving your goals and dreams in the *future*. Because let me assure you—you are not perfect at anything yet! Even most successful people never really see themselves as having reached total perfection in their field. When you see yourself as having reached perfection at something, you stop striving to be better at it, and that is the beginning of becoming worse. Mistakes and failures don't mean that we're bad at something or that we're not making progress at it—rather, they ensure that we realize we still have room for upward growth and improvement. This is a super-valuable frame of mind to have, and you have failure to thank for it—and I think that's pretty great.

To avoid letting your failures rob you of your confidence and belief in your dream, challenge yourself to think about the

positives of moments of failure, even if they might not seem obvious at the time. Additionally, when you start to feel a mistake or failure encroaching on your self-confidence, challenge yourself to think of your failure as something distinct, separate, and different from you! Remember that it is not your failures that define you, but rather how you react to them. Do you get back up again when you've been knocked down? Do you maintain a positive attitude after setbacks? Do you try to learn from your failures and mistakes? These attributes are what will lead you successfully to your dream. Fortitude, perseverance, and certitude are far more important and powerful qualities to have than perfection.

Learn from Other People's Failures!

Here's a secret, from me to you—you don't have to be the one to make every mistake or experience every failure firsthand. You can save yourself a lot of time and angst by learning from the mistakes and failures that *others* have made! I know, I know. Mind. Blown.

Use this activity to practice learning from other people's mistakes, instead of making them all yourself. In the space on the next page, list three people in your field of interest who have made mistakes or failed at something and then answer the questions for each of those people.

The people you choose could be famous people, role models, or people you know personally.

1. _____

2. _____

3. _____

What did each of these people fail at, and how did they fail?

1. _____

2. _____

3. _____

Why did each of these people fail?

1. _____

2. _____

3. _____

What can you learn from these failures/mistakes to improve your own path?

1. _____

2. _____

3. _____

Someone who definitely learned from her failures was Nora Ephron. Ephron was an acclaimed writer of both books and movies (including modern classics like *Sleepless in*

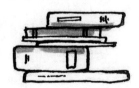

Seattle and *When Harry Met Sally*), but not all of her projects were successful. Over the course of her career, Ephron was nominated for three best director Oscars, and won several other notable awards as well . . . but she also won two Golden Raspberry Awards (also known as Razzies). The Razzies are basically the opposite of the Oscars—they celebrate the *worst* films of the year! Ephron won a Razzie both for worst screenplay and for worst director. *Oof.* But it was through her failures—whether they won awards for being so terrible or just went relatively under the radar—that Ephron was able to continue to grow as a writer and director and to hone her skills to become what we remember her as today: one of the greats.

Get Comfy with Failure Through Practice!

You don't have to wait until you experience a failure to practice reacting to it. The activity on the next page will ask you to do something that (unless you're already pretty experienced at it) will involve failing a couple of times! Consider this a low-stakes and low-stress opportunity to practice growing from failure.

Pick a place that you know the layout of well—for instance, this could be your living room, your backyard, or your bedroom (make sure to pick somewhere without stairs or other hazards that could injure you). Now, try closing your eyes and walking through that place without bumping into anything! That sounds like it should be pretty easy, right? Well . . . maybe not quite as easy as you thought— you might need a couple tries to get it right. Each time you mess up and have to try again, you learn a little something more and you can take that knowledge into your next attempt and eventually get it *just right*. Also, pay attention to the emotions that you feel when something doesn't go quite right—try to keep a positive, learning mindset throughout!

In the space below, sketch out a rough layout of the place that you chose to use for this activity (this sketch doesn't have to be anything special; if you're not great at art, you can just draw squares or rectangles for you bed, dresser, etc.)—then trace the different routes that you took each time and see how much better you got with each try!

Triumph in Failure

I want you to take a minute to think about the greatest success stories out there. Really ask yourself, what are the stories that we remember, the ones that resonate deeply with us? Almost always, they are the stories that include failure as a crucial element prior to success—they are the comeback stories. And some degree of failure has to be wrapped up in them, because you can't have a comeback without a knockdown. The stories of success that inspire us the most are those that include perseverance in the face of failure, and often perseverance in the face of repeated failures. Sure, an accomplishment is celebration-worthy on its own. But an accomplishment after setbacks, disappointments, and all-out failures? That's even more than celebration-worthy—that's legendary.

The reason we love stories with failure in them is that failure is such a universal human experience. We've all experienced it (whether in a small way or on the path to our biggest dreams) and as such, each and every one of us roots for success when it comes around.

Often, when we are in the midst of experiencing a failure, when we're right there in the thick of it, it can be difficult to see how our immediate turmoil might eventually become one of our great points of pride. That makes sense, right? Failure can feel dramatic and disheartening—in the moment, it can feel like the endpoint of a dream. And the more dearly you hold your dream, the more deeply you might feel the setbacks as you work toward it. But if we want to be successful through failure (and even use it to further our dreams instead of ending them), it's important to alter the way that we perceive it. We need to be able to find the triumph that we know is the flip side of the failure coin even as it's happening. To cultivate a mindset to find triumph, not only once you're at a height, but more importantly, while you're at a low point, try to think of the failure that you're experiencing (or have experienced in the past) as a plot point in the story of your dream.

A great way to improve your mindset and find the positive sides of your mistakes and failures is to challenge yourself to place your experiences into a larger perspective. Is the failure that you're currently experiencing *truly* the end of your journey to reach your dream? Or is there a way that you can "rise up from the ashes" and continue on your path with greater focus and drive than before? Our failures and mistakes often seem much larger, worse, and more important at the time that we experience them than they really are. It's often not until some time has passed that we really see how insignificant our missteps might be. If your journey toward your dream is a story, remember that every great story has adversity in it—yours included. But you can and will overcome that adversity! Ask yourself, *If I were telling the story of how I accomplished my dream ten or twenty years from now, how would I talk about this moment of failure?*

Turn Your Failure into a Good Party Story

It can be really hard to see the other side of the rainbow when you are in the midst of experiencing failure. As much as I say that you'll come out fine, or even better, on the other side of this failure, it might be hard for you to actually *feel* that. Use this activity to lighten your mood, place your failure in its eventual context, and find the eventual positive outcomes from your failure (aka, your eventual success)!

Think of something that you've failed at while pursuing your dream (or even something you're worried you might fail at some time in the future). Now imagine that ten years have passed since that failure. You're at a party telling your friends a story about this point in time (or, if you prefer, you're standing on a stage giving a speech about it). In the space below and on the next page, write out the main plot points of the story you would tell about your failure. Imagine how great it will feel to see people react not only to your failure but also to your comeback! Will the story you tell be funny? Sad? Regretful? Triumphant? All of those? Something else entirely? It's up to you—it's your story! Just remember, you may not have experienced the comeback yet, but you will. Make sure to include your epic success in your story. If you're feeling extra ambitious, go past the highlights of your story of failure triumph and write out the full thing!

_____

_____

_____

_____

_____

_____

_____

_____

_____

_____

Success is more meaningful and impactful when it occurs not *without* failure, but *regardless of* failure, or even *because of* failure. Experiencing failure along the road to your dreams helps you develop resiliency and grit—traits that will help you accomplish so much in life. And even more, experiencing failure tells you that you are on the right track—that you are challenging yourself to push your boundaries and truly do something that stretches your limits. If you're not experiencing failure, it just might mean that you're not challenging yourself enough to truly discover your full potential.

You are the only person who gets to decide how you feel and think about a failure—and what's more, you are the only person who gets to decide what even qualifies as a failure, a success,

or something in between! In the same way that not everyone will understand your dream and your dedication to your dream, some people might not understand why you feel the way you do about specific steps along the way. The only opinion that truly matters is your own! Thomas Edison once said, "I have not failed. I've just found 10,000 ways that won't work." Believe in your dream and the path you've chosen to take to accomplish it. Don't limit yourself by letting other people put *their* limits on you! And most importantly, remember that everyone (including you) fails before they can accomplish or achieve anything and it's only through this failure that you can learn and improve. Failure isn't inherently a bad thing; it's an opportunity. So even though it may not always feel so great to fail—in fact, it will probably feel pretty lousy most of the time—failure is an important step in following and achieving your dreams.

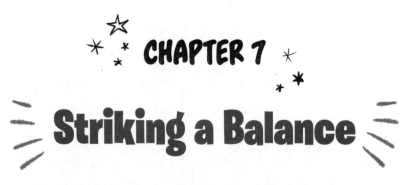

CHAPTER 7

Striking a Balance

Every day is a new day, and ultimately, I have to figure out what works each day.

—Nathan Chen, Olympic bronze medalist
American figure skater

Sometimes you get so excited about something—like chasing after a dream or even just a new experience that you're engaged in—that you lose balance in your life. That was definitely what I did when I first entered college. I remember going to the college activity fair during orientation and signing up for *everything*. Seriously, I went back to my dorm room with dozens of flyers for clubs that I wanted to join, and that was on top of having already joined the diving team, taking a full class load, signing up for violin lessons, joining the campus observatory volunteer group, and so many other new things I've almost lost count. I was just so excited about all the opportunities that were now available to me!

But while each individual opportunity was definitely awesome, it turned out that I had bitten off a bit more than I could chew. I was burning the candle at both ends, not getting nearly enough sleep in order to make time for all of the activities I wanted to do—academics, sports, social life, volunteering—and one morning this caught up with me. I was at a 5:00 a.m. diving practice, definitely too tired, and I messed up a pretty crucial part of a dive I was practicing. I wound up face planting hard in the water, and I gave myself a nice little concussion. As you might imagine, having a concussion during my first year of college really wasn't fun! But the entire episode did help me see that I had been experiencing burnout, and I realized that I needed to have a bit more balance in my life. In fact, I came to learn that having more balance would help me to be happier and healthier in life in general, but also that, without balance, I wouldn't be very successful at chasing after my dream!

When you have a goal and a dream—really, anytime you want something deeply—your first instinct might be to throttle up to 100 percent and work toward accomplishing it nonstop, with all your might. Why not try your hardest at all times? Why not give it your all at every possible opportunity? If that's the attitude that you have about chasing after your dream, you're doing something right—you absolutely should try your hardest and fully commit yourself to achieving your dream. So then, why does it seem like I'm teeing up to say the complete opposite? Well, because I am.

While I'll definitely be the first person to tell you to pursue your dream with all your might, I'll also be the first person to caution you to *not* go from zero to a hundred from the get-go, or to try to maintain that hundred-level pace for the entire time you're making moves toward your dream. Because the bizarre, seemingly self-contradictory truth about chasing after something is that pouring your all into it every single moment can often backfire on you. For anything in our lives, but especially for the things that we care the most about, it's vitally important that we learn how to strike a balance and place things in perspective, and by doing so, avoid outcomes like burnout and regret.

It's not too hard to understand, at a basic level, why balance is important to humans—too much of any one thing, no matter how great that thing is, becomes bad! Imagine only eating candy for the rest of your life—at first that seems like a pretty sweet deal, yeah? But after just a couple of days you'd start getting stomachaches and headaches from all the sugar and losing your taste for the sweetness. After a couple of weeks your skin would start to break out, and your hair and nails would become brittle from lack of nutrients. After a couple of months your bones would deteriorate and your muscles would start to wither away. The way that you spend your time—how much time and on what—has a similar effect, except on your mind instead of your body. If you only focus on one thing (your dream and the efforts involved in chasing after it), you'll find that your determination and even your passion for your dream might start to fade, and possibly disappear altogether. This is known as burnout.

We live in a world and a society that seems to be increasingly fast-paced, overflowing with stimuli, and, overall, more stressful than ever before. Some of the same things that have contributed to the really incredible aspects of the twenty-first century are also what contribute to these downsides. Take personal technology and social media, for example. They ensure that we are constantly connected, which is arguably one of the most powerful innovations for humans ever. But they also ensure that we're constantly inundated with different types of media, different ways to pull our focus and attention, different things to care about or worry about—and a new set of these things comes along every single time we refresh our screens or scroll to a new page. The ever-increasing pace of the world—and our individual lives, which only grow more hectic as time goes on—makes it all the more important to learn and practice striking a balance for ourselves, and to prepare for how to manage when we don't get that balance quite right. That may sound like a lot to figure out right now, but it's totally doable—I promise! Read on for more.

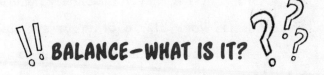

BALANCE—WHAT IS IT?

In this instance, I'm not talking about the kind of balance that has to do with standing on your tiptoe on one foot. It's mental balance that I want to dive into here, and it's just as important as standing upright! Having mental balance means ensuring that the way that you spend your time and energy (neither of which comes in endless supply!) matches up with the values that you hold for your life. What mental balance looks like for each of us is different—because we all have different values and needs for our lives, and different resources available to us to help us reach them. But in general, finding balance involves building strong relationships with the people around you, making time for health and fitness (both physical and mental), and having and engaging in a variety of interests and activities. Another way to think about balance is that it's self-care. This means that a starting point to think about balance is to figure out the answer to this question: What do you absolutely need to have in your life in order to stay happy and healthy, and to continue to be able to reach for your dreams?

Visualize Balance

On one side of the scale below, draw or list the different elements of your dream and what you're doing to achieve it. On the other side, draw or list other activities, interests, and priorities that you have that aren't related to your dream. The goal of striving for balance is to make sure that neither of these plates is weighted down too heavily. If you start to notice that one side is more full than the other— that's okay! The point of this activity isn't to judge yourself or to even make any commentary on your current balance, but just to start thinking about what you have going on in your life and whether or not those things are balanced.

Balance isn't generally something that most people just happen upon. For many of us, it's is a skill that we have to learn and practice, something we need to continually do as we move through life and rethink what's important to us at any given moment. As our lives change, so do the things that we need to do, and are able to do, to find balance. Think of it like juggling all the different things in your life. After a while you'll probably get pretty good at juggling just three things, and you might not even have to consciously think about it to keep going. But what if a fourth thing gets thrown in? Or a fifth? What if the size, shape, or weight of the things that you're juggling changes? What if suddenly you're juggling the life equivalent of flaming torches?! When you think of it that way, you can see why you'd want to be paying attention when these changes happen, and to use different techniques to successfully juggle each of them.

When Do You Feel Balanced?

Fill out the Venn diagram on the next page by listing times when you've felt cared for emotionally, physically, or mentally. If you've felt two of these at the same time, put those moments in the corresponding overlapping area. If you've felt all three at once, put them in the very middle!

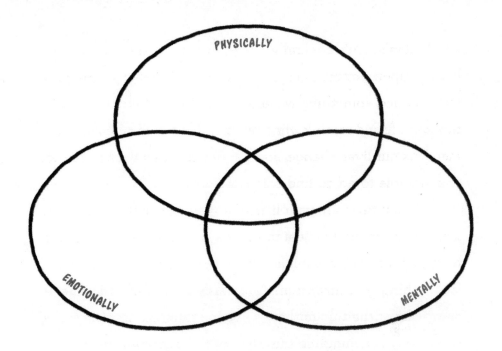

BALANCE—IT'S NOT ALWAYS EASY!

Before we go any further, let me make one thing clear: the idea of a perfectly, completely, and entirely balanced life is a myth, and a harmful one at that! Life is never perfect, and it's also constantly changing. So, know that perfect balance at all moments is not the goal here. But that doesn't mean we shouldn't still strive toward having balance in our lives, and this is especially true as we reach for our dreams. Why? Well, even if you're not perfect at it, having more balance in your life is significantly better for you than having less balance. To go back to the juggling analogy, it's easier to try to figure out a new juggling method each time another ball is added than to wait until you suddenly have ten balls that you have to keep in the air and no practice at juggling more than three, right? You can trust me about that, I used to be in the circus. (Seriously, it's true—but that's a story for another day.) Striving for balance is like a tool that helps you be the best version of yourself that you can possibly be.

Sometimes finding or working toward balance will go against what you think you're supposed to be doing. The society that we live in places a really high value on people who "Go! Go! Go!" all the time and doesn't necessarily place as much value on slowing down and doing things in good time. But in most cases, chasing after a dream is a marathon, not a sprint. I know that's something that people say a lot, but it's true. In the long run, taking a break or slowing down isn't a bad thing, or a shameful thing—it actually shows that you know how to take care of yourself, which will be crucial for your future success!

One of the difficulties that comes with trying to find a good life balance is that you might have to make hard choices in the short term to benefit your long-term success. You may have to give up something that you like right now in order to have the time and energy to stay the course toward your long-term dream. Or you may have to slow down in your efforts to reach your dream to make enough time for the other important facets of your life. Or maybe you'll find some sort of solution in the middle, where you get to keep all of the things in your life but spend less time and effort on some or all of them. And

that's okay! You don't have to—and in fact, you really shouldn't try to—do everything or be perfect at everything that you do. And whichever way you go about trying to find balance, know that you might have to change course along the way to figure out which works best for you.

STRIKE A BALANCE BETWEEN YOUR LIFE AND YOUR DREAM

Finding a balance might be difficult, but I think we can all agree that it's worth it, right? And in fact, there are a few things you can already start to do to strike a balance between working toward your dream and managing anything else you have going on. Spending the time to do this now, and getting into the habit of finding balance, will pay off immensely all the way along your path toward your dream! It's all about being self-aware: knowing what's most important to you, what's absolutely necessary for you, and what you have at hand to help out in both categories.

WHAT'S MOST IMPORTANT TO YOU?

Knowing what's important to you means taking an honest look at your life and clearly defining your values and priorities. Those will definitely be different for each of us on a specific level, but there are some bigger-picture concepts that many of us share. Those might include family, education, goals and dreams, fun and enjoyment, and communal good. Some of these things might be on your list of things you value and prioritize—but don't worry if some or even all of them aren't on your list, or if something that you value wasn't on that list. Each of our lists will look different, and it's up to you to figure out what makes sense to be on yours.

What Do You Value?

It's possible (and more common than not) to have multiple different things in your life that you value. But you might not value each thing the exact same amount. Some things are just more important to us than others—and what those things are are different for each and every one of us. In the space on the next page, make a list of the things that are important in your life. Here are some examples of the different kinds of things you might write down, just to help get your brain moving: family/time with your family, friends/your social life, school (or even a specific subject or class at school that you really enjoy), unstructured free time, dating, self-care, physical fitness, time alone, creativity, religion. Don't worry if your list looks pretty different from this set of examples—remember that you and your dream are unique individuals! Try to include some things that

you value that are important to your overall life, and some that are important because of your dream! For example, a dream-specific item I would include in my list is having regular access to clear, dark skies for stargazing. What are your dream-specific items?

After you've made your list, go back through it and put a star or a smiley face next to the things that jump out to you as most important.

_____   _____

_____   _____

_____   _____

_____   _____

                                _____

Part of determining what's important to you—and therefore finding balance in your life—is learning to not compare yourself (your abilities, needs, or limits) to anybody else! We are all unique individuals, with unique dreams and circumstances. What you need to do—and what you're capable of doing—to be both healthy and happy in the short term and accomplish your dream in the long run will be different from what anyone else needs to do to accomplish theirs.

Imagine a friend of yours on a sports team that you're both a part of. Let's say that friend practices for five hours a day, every day of the week. Does that mean that you should do the same? No! Just because that works for your friend doesn't mean that it would work well for you. You might be physically different from your friend, and that much time practicing would be too hard on your body, whereas they feel like they really need it to succeed. Or maybe you have other things in your life that you'd rather focus your time and energy on, and your dream doesn't have anything to do with the sport that the two of you play!

This idea of not comparing yourself to others doesn't just hold true for the hypothetical example above—it's also true for every part of your life. Part of finding balance is being able to recognize what the reality of your life is (such as how much time you have, or what other resources you have available), not what you wish your reality was or what anyone else thinks your current state is! This doesn't mean that you can't grow in the future, but you can't serve yourself well if you aren't self-aware. Just the way you are is exactly how you should be right now! Don't try to be anyone else but yourself.

Determine Your Basic Needs

The next piece of the puzzle is to know what your needs are—the things you truly need to get by. Each and every one of us has needs, and if we don't get what we need to fulfill them, we stop functioning at our best. It's significantly harder to chase after your dream if you aren't first aware of, and meeting, your needs.

The basic needs that all humans share include things like sleeping enough (and making sure that sleep is good quality),

eating enough (and eating nutritious foods), drinking enough water, getting physical exercise on a regular basis, spending time around other people, having emotional connections and bonds with other humans, and experiencing stimulating and varied environments.

Sleep is truly one of the most important basic needs that you have, and it's one that's often overlooked. Getting enough sleep, and getting that sleep on a regular schedule, helps us maintain a more positive state of mind and be more creative, focused, and productive. Sleep helps your brain to process memories and store information, repair damage throughout the body, and so much more (lots of which we don't even fully understand yet!). But as positive as getting enough quality sleep can be, not

getting enough can be significantly more harmful. Short-term sleep deprivation can cause things like mental fog (including issues with memory, concentration, and alertness), as well as irritability, migraines, lack of motivation, and more. Long-term or chronic sleep deprivation can cause all of these problems, plus it can increase your risk of developing dangerous health conditions such as diabetes and heart disease. And if you don't sleep for long enough in a row (eleven days on average, to be specific), it can literally kill you!

So, as you can see, sleep is a pretty important basic need for humans. But how much sleep do you need to be healthy and productive? Well, the precise amount is different for everyone based on a number of factors, including your genes and how active you tend to be, but the recommended amount for people between the ages of seven to twelve is ten to eleven hours per night. For people between the ages of twelve to eighteen that number drops, but only a bit, to eight to ten hours. All of which is to say: to find your balance and reach for your dream, make sure you get enough sleep!

The foods we eat, the liquids we drink, and the frequency with which we exercise can also greatly contribute to our ability to achieve our goals, both short- and long-term. Eating a diet low in the necessary nutrients, being dehydrated, and not exercising on a regular basis can cause us to both not feel well enough to continue chasing after our dreams on a day-to-day basis and run the risk for health complications and diseases in the long term. And all three can drastically affect our mental health as well! Think about your own personal experiences with what you eat and drink, and how often you exercise—do certain things make you feel overall better, and as such more interested in and able to chase after your dream, than others? Do you feel more alert after eating a particular food, or more focused after a burst of physical activity? While our diet and exercise needs are bound to be different for each of us, there are some general guidelines that we can all count on. Those include aiming to eat a wide variety of foods, drinking enough water every day, limiting our intake of sugary foods and beverages, and exercising on a regular basis in a way that feels both physically challenging and mentally satisfying!

One other basic need that we all, as humans, share is the need for community. Humans are inherently social beings, and as such absolutely require and rely on strong relationships and regular contact with other humans. This is just as true for introverts (people who tend to keep to themselves a bit more) as it is for extroverts (people who tend to be more outgoing), even if to different degrees! Isolation can cause serious damage to our mental health, and can lead to things like depression, lack of motivation, and decreased creativity—none of which are conducive to living a balanced, dream-reaching life! And having a community of people who know you and care about you not only has a direct impact on your health—it also serves as a warning system and a safety net. In some instances, you might not be able to see that your own life is unbalanced, or that you're moving in the direction of a burnout, and the people who are close to you might be able to see and help nudge you in the right direction. If you do wind up in a situation where you're struggling or burning out along the road to achieving your dream, it's this same group of people who will be there to support you and help you get back up on your feet and in the game.

Each of these basic human needs seems simple enough on its own, right? Even thinking about all of them together feels just like talking about normal parts of life. But when we become stressed out, overly anxious, or short on time—all of which might happen as we chase after our dreams full-speed—it's incredibly easy to lose track of how important these are. It can be tempting to sacrifice any of these things in exchange for more time, or even just as a byproduct of anxiety. I guarantee you that these things make up the base of your balance in life, and your ability to chase after your dream, so please think twice before you make tradeoffs with them!

Make Your Own Hierarchy of Needs

Fill out the pyramid on the next page with your own personal hierarchy of needs. They might include the three things we just talked

about, but they might also include other things that are more specific to you, like spending time snuggling your cat or practicing a certain skill (drawing, singing, sports, etc.) on a regular basis. Fill the bottom section with the things that are most important to your ability to continue functioning well on a day-to-day basis—or that you need the most of to do just that. With each section up, fill in things that are important to you but maybe a bit less so than the ones in the level below, until you reach the top.

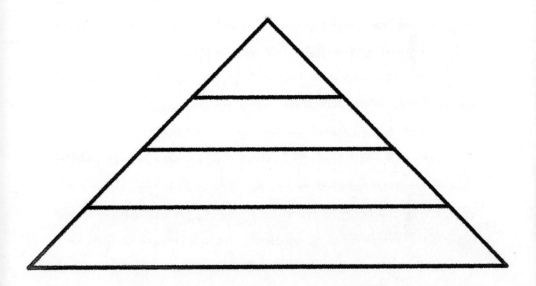

DEFINE YOUR RESOURCES

We've talked about figuring out what's important to you, as well as what's truly vital to you. Now try to extend your self-awareness a little bit further out. Think beyond your values and priorities, and even beyond your basic needs—think about what you have on hand that helps ensure that you can maintain all of those things. Ask yourself, *What resources do I have available that allow me to pursue my priorities and enable me to get the things I need?* Identifying and using these resources well can help bring balance to your life, and as such, set you up to chase after your dream!

Here's something to remember when thinking about these resources: they can be things that you see around you, external resources like your family or community, your ability to access certain tools, or even your favorite food. But they can also be internal, things that you have as part of yourself, like your talents and skills, your growth mindset, and your resiliency and grit. Hopefully you'll find that you have some combination of both internal and external resources at your disposal!

Once you've taken stock of what your resources are, think about how much of each you have. Chances are, you don't have all of them in a completely unlimited supply! So it's time to ask yourself, *How can I most efficiently use these resources?* Have you ever heard the phrase "Work smarter, not harder"? Well, if not, you have now! It's one of my favorite phrases. Working smarter, not harder, means looking for ways that you can use your resources more efficiently, whatever they may be, to accomplish more while using up less. Essentially, you're looking for ways that you can take shortcuts without losing quality. I think that you'll find that in many parts of your life, there are ways to change how you do something so that it takes less

time, energy, or any other resource. All it takes is some forethought and creativity to figure these changes out. Here are a couple of my favorite ways to work smarter, not harder.

One way is by setting up a habit or routine for my average day, including all of my everyday activities. For you these activities might include things like brushing your teeth, packing your lunch, or doing your homework at the same time and same place after school. The point of a routine isn't to trap you into doing the same things every single day—it's actually to give you the freedom to do more of what you want to! If you can put your brain on automatic for these types of everyday things, you don't have to think about them as often and therefore can have more brainpower and energy to focus on your dream.

I also like to make "to-don't lists." You're probably familiar with to-do lists—but you might not have heard of the to-don't list yet! A to-don't list is a list of all the things that you don't necessarily want to spend your time or energy doing. For example, your to-don't list might include things like checking social media frequently if you know that that takes up a lot of your time, or deciding that a specific task or chore (such as organizing your room) is not on your agenda for the day.

Elite figure skater **Nathan Chen** knows a thing or two about finding balance—and not just when he's landing the quadruple jumps on ice that he's famous for! Nathan is a two-time world champion skater, a four-

time US champion skater, a performer in the touring Stars on Ice show, a member or the US Olympic team, and . . . somehow he's also an undergraduate student at Yale University! An injury from skating in 2016 made him rethink his single-minded commitment to the sport and inspired him to pursue growth in other parts of his life as well—namely, in academics. But that doesn't mean that he's given up on his figure-skating dream. Nathan balances training for competitions with his Ivy League classes by carefully prioritizing his health, frequently reassessing his resources and his needs and goals, working with people who support him, and using creative time management. For example, Nathan practices on the hockey rink at Yale so that he doesn't have to spend time commuting to an off-campus figure-skating rink. He also works remotely with his coach, who lives in California full-time! Just like Nathan, creative use of your resources and creative time management can help you strike a winning balance in your dream—and your life!

Resource Management on the Brain

One resource that we all have only a limited supply of is our ability to focus on many things at once. Essentially, we only have so much space in our brains! Divide up the drawing of the brain on the next page into sections of different sizes for the various needs or priorities in your life, and label each section based on how much brainpower you'd ideally like to spend on each of them.

One pro tip about using your resources to the best of your abilities is to be selective about what you agree to do. Of course, I'm not suggesting that you stop doing things you want to do, or that you say no to helping other people. What I am recommending is that you set healthy boundaries around what you will and won't spend your time on. Don't be a "yes person" (someone who agrees to things that others ask of them immediately, and without regard to their actual capability to fulfill the obligation). It's okay to not immediately commit to a request from someone else for your time—simply tell the person asking you for help, time, or any other resource that you have that you are focusing on living a balanced life and need some time to think about how their request will fit into your life. This might not be something that you can do now—depending on how old you are, or any number of other factors, you might not really get to choose all of the things that you do on a daily basis. Even if that's the case, though, it's a pretty important skill to learn now so that you can use it in the future when you have more options of what you choose to do!

Ultimately, managing your resources well and being aware of what you have is incredibly important for dreamers. Working toward your dream can be difficult and time consuming, and will probably keep you pretty busy, at least some of the time. Keeping track of your priorities, your needs, and your resources can help you maintain your balance as you go, which will undoubtedly help you as you move down the path toward your dream.

WHAT IS BURNOUT?

Remember that feeling of burnout that we talked about at the start of this chapter, when you just feel so exhausted or overwhelmed that you lose your energy and drive toward your dream? Sometimes, no matter how hard you try to balance your life to keep on track as you reach toward your dream, you might still encounter it. In fact, it's pretty likely that at some point in your life you'll experience burnout at some level! Burnout happens most often when you're under too much stress for too long of a period of time. And while chasing after our dreams is a really great and powerful thing, it can also place stress on us— worrying about not achieving your dream can be stressful, as can constantly having things to check off on a to-do list.

Your specific dream might also have its own particular stresses associated with it. For example, even though I love public speaking, I still feel a fair amount of stress and anxiety when I prepare for a big speech or presentation. All of these stresses associated with having and chasing after your dream, in addition to the various stresses that life already holds, can become too much sometimes. As with most things in life, there are positives and negatives to being a dreamer—and the potential for experiencing heightened stress and burnout is sometimes the flip side of the excitement of reaching for your dreams.

Not only does burnout happen more often to dreamers and doers, but it can also be more frustrating to these same groups of people. You might feel guilt, anger, shame, or other negative emotions if you're experiencing burnout, and therefore become too exhausted, distracted, or inefficient to make progress toward your dream. Burnout can also be an especially frustrating experience if you're used to setting goals and then crushing them. If you're used to being self-motivated and productive, becoming unmotivated, uninspired, or unproductive can not only feel frustrating but also confusing!

One of the things that can make burnout such a confusing experience is that sometimes you might not even realize that that's what's going on! Instead, you might attribute your negative emotions, lack of interest, and other symptoms to no longer having a passion for or interest in your dream. On the contrary, though—experiencing burnout definitely does *not* mean that you're no longer passionate and dedicated to your dream (and it also doesn't mean that you're not suited for or won't be successful at your dream). It actually might mean the opposite—that you love your dream so much that you lost focus of your balance in life because of it!

Burnouts can be caused by any number of things, but here are a few of the most common risk factors to avoid:

✔️ *Not managing something that's stressing you out—either because you don't recognize what's causing your stress or because you don't realize how harmful long-term stress can be!*

(✔) *Not making enough time to spend focused on yourself. One of the main culprits that can cause this is being constantly connected to the world at large through technology and social media. This type of constant connection means that you're always "on" and don't end up getting any real breaks from your responsibilities and stresses.*

(✔) *Not feeling in control of your life, or feeling like things are spiraling out of your control.*

(✔) *Having set expectations that are just too high, whether they come from yourself or from others. Remember a few chapters back when you looked at your dream and broke it up into smaller, more manageable steps? Well, not doing so, or not breaking it up into small enough or achievable enough steps can contribute to burning out before you achieve your dream.*

(✔) *Even just having too much on your plate over a long period of time, especially with no end to that load in sight, can cause enough stress and lead to burnout!*

An important thing to know about burnout is that it really doesn't matter how big or stressful your dream or your life may seem to anyone else. You can experience burnout while chasing after a dream of any size, as long as it's important to you!

How to Bounce Back After Burnout

When burnout hits, it can affect your physical health, your mental health, and even your emotional stability. But don't worry, if burnout does happen to you, it's completely manageable with the right knowledge and skills. First and foremost you have to be able to recognize if and when you're experiencing burnout. This can be a little bit tricky, because burnout can look and feel very different to different people. But there are a few signs to look for that are common for many people experiencing burnout:

* *Getting sick frequently, or experiencing a major and unexpected health issue associated with stress.*
* *Decreased capability—at school, at home, at sports/band/robotics/any other activity.*
* *An unusual level of moodiness and disinterest in your usual activities.*
* *Feeling increasingly on edge, which might play out by getting angry at people around you or upset by little things that you'd normally just brush off.*

Even if your burnout doesn't exactly mirror one of the reactions listed above, you can still use these as references to recognize a burnout that's playing out in a slightly different (but still related) way. Burnouts can have many other symptoms as well, but those will usually be in addition to (or even caused by) one of the signs listed above. So try to keep an eye out for these types of reactions as you chase after your dream, and if you see them happening, take a step back and think about whether you might need a bit more balance in your life!

Once you do experience—and recognize that you're experiencing—burnout, it's up to you to get through it! Here are some tips and techniques on how you can bounce back and find your ideal balance again:

- ✦ *Take a break from your dream. Intentionally put it on hiatus for a while. But before you do so, make a plan for how and when you're going to get back to chasing after it. Making a plan like this is important for a couple of reasons: First off, it will help you to not feel like you've failed at your dream (which you haven't!). Secondly, having a plan for how and when you'll start working toward your dream again ensures that you don't let it fade away or fall to the wayside while you're taking your vacation from it. Here are some suggestions of things to do during your break from your dream:*

  o Spend time with people you care about—and who care about you. Nothing is more revitalizing to the human spirit than spending quality time with others. Spend some extra time with your favorite people—friends, family, teammates, whoever you'd like—not focused on or involved in your dream at all.

o Do something that you know that you enjoy. What this is will be different for each and every one of us, but the idea is to pick an activity that's not related to your dream that you *know* brings you joy or comfort. For example, when I'm feeling overwhelmed or burned out, I like to paint, dance, bake, or even take a bubble bath! In fact, I relied on this technique so much during college that my friends and professors could always tell when I was feeling overly stressed or overextended because I would show up with fresh baked goods. I call that stress baking, and for me, it's a win-win way to manage stress.

o Flex your creative muscles. One of the most unifying human qualities is creativity—it's something that has driven humanity for our entire history. Whether or not you know it, feel it, or believe it, you—yes you—have the ability to be creative. Creativity isn't the same thing as expertise—when I say to flex your creative muscles I don't mean that you have to create a work of art on the level of Frida Kahlo, Picasso, or Salvador Dalí. Creativity is about doing, not producing. The creativeness that you practice doesn't have to be for anyone else to consume but you. You really don't have to be good at something to do it. Like to paint even though your paintings tend to come out looking more like splatters than anything else? Doesn't matter, do it anyway! Like to dance even though you think you're uncoordinated? Never mind, dance away! You get the idea: the only thing that matters when it comes to creative activities is that you enjoy them. And thankfully, there is an infinite number of different ways to be creative, so I'm sure that there's something out there that you'll enjoy doing. Spending some time playing with your creative side can help you feel more inspired, develop personal satisfaction, and reduce stress—basically, it's like hitting the reset button on your brain so that you can get back to chasing after your dream!

o   Try something completely new. Much like flexing your creative muscles, trying something that you've never done before can both be a palate cleanser for your brain and provide you with some much-needed stimulus. This new thing could be something very small, such as reading a book in a different genre from your usual taste, or something large, such as learning a new language.

✕   *Feel your emotions fully, without shaming yourself, placing judgment on yourself, or boxing yourself in at all. Essentially, give yourself the permission to feel whatever it is that you're feeling at the time, rather than focusing on what you think you should be feeling. If you're feeling tired, let yourself feel tired. If you're feeling angry, fully feel that anger. If you're sad, give yourself time to grieve. The only way to get past these emotions and get back to chasing* after your dream is to truly deal with them, and the only way to do that is by experiencing them fully and without judgment. There is nothing wrong with feeling burned out, tired, sad, or any other negative emotion—these are all feelings that are part of being human and that come along with caring about something deeply, like how you care about your dream. To fully experience an emotion and deal with it in a healthy way, consider these techniques:

o   Try talking about your feelings/situation with a friend, mental-health-care professional, or other trusted person in your life.

o   Try to place your feelings into words—consider talking to yourself in the mirror or journaling about what you're feeling and why you think you're feeling it. Remember, it's completely okay to have a feeling but not be able to put your finger on quite why you feel that way—in such instances, knowing that you're not sure what the cause is can be helpful.

o   Treat yourself and your emotions with kindness. It can be easy to judge ourselves harshly for feeling emotions such as burnout or exhaustion, but doing so definitely won't help you deal with your emotions in a healthy way. Practice treating yourself with kindness when you're feeling down by giving advice on your situation/emotions but pretending that it's actually your best friend's situation that you're advising on! Would you have the same negative things to say to them as you might to yourself, or would you be more understanding and forgiving to them?

✗ ***Broaden your perspective.*** *It can be easy when you're experiencing burnout to feel like the world is narrowing in around you and to lose your perspective of what's important. There are a few ways you can go about broadening your perspective that can help you get over the hump of a burnout:*

o Reflect back on why you were so passionate about your dream in the first place. What made you set out on this journey? Why did it used to be important to you? Do you have any materials (such as journal pages, plans, goal sheets, videos, drawings, etc.) from when you were first setting out on your journey to achieve your dream that you can reflect back on? Doing so might help rekindle that fire inside you that drove you to reach for your dream in the first place!

o Remember what you value, and why. If you're finding yourself undergoing burnout, it's likely because you're experiencing a lack of balance either in your life as a whole or specifically with your dream. Reevaluating your priorities (what's most important in your life, what you need to be happy and healthy, and the resources that you have available to meet both of these categories) can help you find balance again and get back on track. If you're not really sure how to reevaluate, try revisiting the activities from earlier on in this chapter!

o   Project yourself into the future and think about what will be most important to you down the line. What things will you remember? What will you regret doing—or not doing? What will give you pride in ten, twenty, or even fifty years?

o   Get someone else's opinion! Sometimes when we're experiencing a burnout, we're just too close to it to have a full perspective. When it feels really easy to give up on your dream and you can't quite muster the strength to keep going on or remember why you were so passionate about your dream in the first place, that's a good time to lean on people in your community. Think of your friends, role models, mentors—anyone who is familiar with you and your dream—and talk to them about how you're feeling. You may be surprised by the perspective they're able to share.

It's important to remember that the ideas above are not quick and simple fixes for burnout. Burnout doesn't generally happen because of one specific cause and effect, and as such, it's unlikely that you'll be able to move past it by taking just one action, making just one change in your life, or only working to fix one particular issue. Recovering from burnout—or even avoiding it in the first place—requires a fully balanced approach to life and your dream!

Have Your Pie (Chart) and Eat It Too!

Unless you've discovered time travel (and if you have, let me in on that!), we each only have 24 hours a day and 365.25 days per year. But what's different for each of us is what we consider important, and therefore how we choose to spend the hours and days that we have. Think about how you spend your time, and how you'd ideally like to spend your time, keeping in mind the concepts of balance we've been focusing on in this chapter! Turn the two blank circles on the next page into pie charts. Fill out the first one as a realistic representation of how you spend your time right now. For example, your circle might be broken down into one-third sleeping, one-quarter at school or studying, an eighth eating, a quarter playing sports or hanging out with friends, a sliver watching TV, and so on. It's up to you! Try to be as accurate as you can about how you spend your time, but remember that these are just estimates—you don't need to track your every moment. Then fill out the second circle with an idealistic representation of how you'd like to spend your time, focusing on finding the right balance for you and your dream!

Preventing or bouncing back from burnout requires maintaining self-awareness and self-reflection, investing in a well-rounded and balanced life, and remembering to enjoy life at every step along the way. While it can be tempting to want to go full steam ahead with your dream (trust me, I understand that

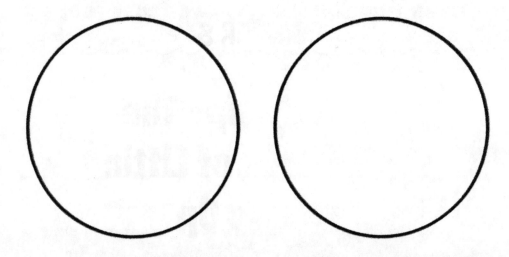

feeling!), as you've just read, that might not actually be the best way to achieve it. It's incredibly hard—and definitely harder than it has to be—to chase after a dream if you're not taking care of yourself along the way. Finding balance by understanding your needs, priorities, and resources, and making a plan for how you'll meet them, will help you stay motivated, inspired, and excited about your dream as you chase after it.

CHAPTER 8

Mentorship—the Importance of Lifting People Up

Show me a successful individual and I'll show you someone who had real positive influences in his or her life. I don't care what you do for a living—if you do it well, I'm sure there was someone cheering you on or showing the way. A mentor.

—Denzel Washington, actor

Easily the most incredible element of my journey to someday become an astronaut has been the people I've met and interacted with along the way. As cheesy as that may sound, I guarantee you that the experiences that you have with (and because of!) other people will be more helpful as you reach for your dream than any material thing possibly could be. We *all* need help throughout life in general, but this is especially true when chasing after our dreams. We absolutely can't do everything on our own, and even when we can accomplish things alone, it's often more effective, more efficient, and overall just better to work with others.

Knowing that we all need help to reach our dreams is important, and it's just as important to know that, in order to get help, we have to know how to ask for it and be able to accept it. Truly, the people that you involve in your aspirations will be central to whether or not you succeed. This is why it's so important to make a conscious effort to attract positive and supportive people into your life. The lessons and skills from chapter 2 ("Be Loud, Be Proud!") were a good start on how to find your community and share your dream—and your path toward it—with others, but this chapter is going to take that idea one step further. Here, we'll narrow it down even more and focus in on a specific subset of people to be loud and be proud about your dream with—mentors!

WHAT'S A MENTOR?

You've probably heard the term "mentor" before. A mentor is a person you admire and look up to, someone who takes a personal interest in you and your dream. A mentor helps guide and advise you over a long period of time. You might be thinking,

Wait, that sounds a lot like a coach or a role model! There can certainly be some overlap, but generally speaking, there are big differences between the three. A coach is someone whose job it is to help teach or train you (sometimes on your own and sometimes as part of a larger group) in a specific skill, usually for a finite period of time. A mentor, on the other hand, is more like someone who has volunteered to help you, and there's usually no set start or finish date for a mentorship. A role model is someone you admire and look up to—someone you might even wish you were like—but who isn't necessarily involved in your life or focused on helping you achieve your dream. In fact, it's not unusual to have role models you've never even met! Unlike a role model, a mentor is someone you get to know personally.

Coaches, role models, and mentors are three distinct types of people you can have in your life. The differences between each of them can get a little bit muddled at times, and that is A-okay. You might even end up seeing one of your coaches or role models become your mentor over time! I've personally had that happen on multiple occasions, and it's really cool—not to mention fulfilling—when it does.

The whole idea of mentorship is that you don't have to "go it alone" as you chase after your dream. A mentor (or better yet, mentors!) can help you believe in yourself and your dream, find and stay on the best path to reach it, and provide critical advice and support along the way. They help you get things done so that you can accomplish your goals and dreams better, more

efficiently, and with less struggle. The ways that mentors can help you are wide and varied, but generally speaking, one of the great advantages of having a mentor is that they can provide you with access to helpful things you might not be able to reach on your own—or that you might not even know existed in the first place—or at the very least, they can guide you on ways to find those things. Mentors, for example, might be able to help you find:

* People to talk to and opportunities to pursue as you chase your dream

* Expert knowledge on the various parts of your dream

* Experience—including both successes and mistakes/ failures that relate to your dream and other people who have pursued something similar

* Specific resources, materials, or facilities—the things you'll need to make your dream happen

- A different perspective from your own, which is always helpful
- Access to a time in history when you might not have even existed yet!

A couple of years ago I had the opportunity to experience both how a role model can become a mentor and how a mentor can be incredibly helpful. Buckle up, it's actually a really funny story! I'd been doing space and science outreach and advocacy work for a few years, and had just recently launched my non-profit, The Mars Generation (TMG). I was excited to see that there was some *buzz* about TMG in the space community, but I'd had no idea how far the news of what I was doing was actually spreading.

One uneventful day, while I was sitting in my college library, I got a phone call. I didn't recognize the number, so I assumed it was someone trying to sell me on something and hit decline. The same number then tried to call me twice more—and I remember thinking that it must have been quite a persistent telemarketer, because I honestly didn't know anyone who still made phone calls out of the blue! About twenty minutes later, I got an email from someone I knew in the space industry, and the email basically said: "WHAT'S GOING ON??? BUZZ FREAKING ALDRIN, THE SECOND PERSON TO WALK ON THE MOON, IS TRYING TO CALL YOU TO TALK AND HE SAYS YOU KEEP HANGING UP ON HIM!!!!!!!" That's right, I had hung up on Buzz Aldrin three times because I thought he was a telemarketer. Oof . . .

Buzz Aldrin, one of only twelve people to have ever walked on the moon, was astronomically high up on my list of role models, and he was calling me up out of the blue! Thankfully, I was able to call him back—and he wasn't too peeved about being ignored repeatedly. He'd called to thank me for my efforts to engage my generation in space exploration through TMG, and to give me some advice about my future aspirations. He was even generous enough to spend the next couple of hours telling me stories from his time in NASA in the sixties and seventies. Since then, I've had the chance to meet Buzz in person a couple of times, and he remains a role model and mentor who I feel fortunate to have learned from.

Mentors are usually people in your field of interest who have more experience than you. But as with so many of the concepts we've discussed in this book, there are no hard and fast rules here. Any number of people can become great mentors to you—it all depends on your unique situation! And you don't have to limit yourself to having just one mentor—the number of mentors you have in your life depends on you, your dream, and your particular journey to reach that dream. Throughout your life you'll probably have many different mentors—as you grow and change over time, so will the mentors who are a part of your life. Mentors are there to help you learn how to navigate that journey and be your best self, in whatever situation that self might be.

FINDING YOUR MENTOR(S) ⚡

It's easy enough to accept the idea that you're likely better off with a mentor (or a couple of 'em!) in your corner. Mentors are great! That said, how exactly do you go about finding someone who will be a good mentor for you and your particular dream?

It might seem a bit daunting when you first start to think about finding a mentor. Perhaps you have too many options—the world is your oyster—and you can't narrow it down or decide who would truly be the best fit. Or perhaps you can't think of very many people who fit the bill and who you have access to in the first place. Maybe the whole idea of starting a mentorship fills you with anxiety and trepidation! And how do you find someone who not only seems like they would make a great mentor from your perspective, but also *wants* to be a mentor, and wants to mentor you? Searching for, and choosing, an appropriate mentor can be a difficult task.

But don't worry! It truly isn't impossible, and really doesn't even have to be all that stressful. I'm not going to tell you that it will always be easy to find a mentor, but I will tell you this—I'm here to make sure it's as easy-breezy as possible! What you're about to read will help you think about what general qualities to look for in a potential mentor, where to look for and find a mentor, and how to choose a mentor who will be able to support you as you reach for your dream.

But before we get to all of that good stuff, there are two

quick but important things to note about mentorships. First off, not every dreamer and their dream need a mentor. Off the bat, this statement might sound contradictory—didn't this whole chapter start out with me telling you how important mentors would be to your dream? While that's true in the majority of cases, it (like many things) is definitely not an absolute. And even though some dreams, and some portions of the journey toward reaching a dream, definitely don't need a mentor, all dreams still need community. The people around you will still be immensely helpful to your journey, even if they're not actually direct mentors.

So if this chapter hasn't really struck a chord with you so far, that's okay! We're all individuals, and all unique in how we go about chasing after our dreams. In some instances it really might not make much sense to look for a mentor. In other cases, you might be at the wrong point on your journey for a mentor to help out. It's been my experience that *most* dreamers are helped by having mentors, but that certainly doesn't mean that that's true for all dreamers and their dreams. Don't force it, and don't worry if finding or having a mentor doesn't feel right to you, now or ever.

And second, while so far I've talked mostly about you finding and benefitting from a mentor, it's important to remember that potential mentors are under no obligation to mentor you. I don't say this to discourage you from seeking them out in any way, but to stress the fact that anyone who becomes a mentor is taking an extra step in helping you. They're going beyond their call of duty, and don't *owe* you their time, energy, or anything else. I truly believe that many people will want to mentor you, because so many people are happy to share their wisdom and expertise with people eager to follow in their footsteps, but please don't forget that having a mentor is a great privilege and opportunity—and remember to always treat your mentors with the respect and appreciation they deserve.

What Makes a Good Mentor?

Before you go looking for a mentor, it helps to know both what makes for a good mentor, generally speaking, and also what you're looking for in a mentor who can help you reach for your particular dream. Regardless of what your dream is, or what path you take to reach it, there are a few staple ideas about mentors that can help you find and choose the best mentor for you.

Your mentor should be someone . . .

1. **Who wants to help you succeed.** That seems pretty basic, right? Well, it is. And that's why it's such an important consideration when searching for a mentor. A real interest in your success is the foundation upon which the rest of your mentor-mentee relationship will be built, so make sure it's strong!

2. **Who has the time necessary to mentor you in the way that you want to be mentored.** It's possible that, in your search for a mentor (or even just in the course of working toward your dream), you might connect with someone amazing, someone who has the best intentions and wants to help you and see you succeed. But if that person just doesn't have the time available to offer the support and guidance that you need, they likely won't make for a great mentor. This doesn't mean that a potential mentor has to have tons of free time, but they do have to have enough time to become invested enough in you.

3. **Who you feel comfortable talking honestly with.** Your mentor needs to be someone you can relate to and share your progress with. If you can't talk candidly with your mentor about your dream and your actions toward it, how are they supposed to offer guidance and support that fit you? Don't worry if you don't feel completely comfortable right at the beginning of your relationship with a mentor—it's completely normal to develop this comfort as you get to know them more fully—but as you look for mentors, remember to think about whether any given person is someone you think you'll be able to develop this comfort with.

4. **Who pushes you outside of your comfort zone.** While it's important to feel comfortable enough with your mentor to be honest with them, it's equally important that your mentor is  someone who will be honest with you as well. There are plenty of people who won't tell you when they disagree with you, or won't tell you hard truths, because they are worried about hurting your feelings or otherwise having difficult conversations. A good mentor is someone who is able to find the right balance to be both supportive and honest with you.

5. **Who has the ability to understand the field that your dream is in.** A mentor by no means needs to be someone who has significant experience in your field of interest (in fact, they don't even have to be in your field at all!), but they do need to be capable of understanding the particulars of your dream in order to give good advice and guidance. This is one of the reasons why having multiple mentors in different areas of your life, each with different backgrounds and different specialties, can be so powerful!

6. **Whose opinion you respect.** Overall, you are the one who gets to make the decisions about your dream and the actions you'll take to reach that dream. A mentor is there to advise and guide you, not to make those decisions for

you. As such, you don't always have to agree with your mentor or do everything that they say. But if you don't respect their opinion, what's the point of enlisting them in the first place? Make sure your mentor is someone whose ideas you give serious consideration to, whether or not you choose to follow all, any, or none of them.

7. **Who has experiences in life that you value.** One of the incredible things about having a mentor is that you get access to their past experiences—their success and failures, their struggles and challenges, their mistakes, and much more. These are the things that will shape how your mentor advises and guides you (as well as what they can advise and guide you on), so make sure that you take the time to really look into your mentor's history before you approach them! It might even be helpful to think about someone whose life experiences don't entirely match your own, so that they can offer a different perspective.

Just as important as knowing the qualities that might make someone a good mentor is knowing about a few qualities that might seem promising—but that do *not* automatically make someone a mentor. Those include: being successful in a particular field, having more experience than you do, holding a senior and/or leadership role, being a role model, being older than you are, or giving out advice. There is no magic formula here, but while great mentors can have some or even all of these attributes, the mere fact that someone has them isn't enough. At the end of the day, a great mentor is simply someone who fits well with their mentee.

Both you and your potential mentor bear the responsibility to think carefully about whether or not you'll be a good match. But ultimately, it's you, your life, and your dream that will be affected the most by having a poorly matched mentor, so think carefully about the qualities listed above. While all of these qualities are important, some may end up being more meaningful and helpful to you. Regardless, it's definitely good to be aware of them all!

Denzel Washington is known worldwide as a talented actor, director, and producer. But what you might not have been aware of is that he's also a dedicated community member, very keen on the importance of giving and receiving mentorship. He serves as the national spokesperson for the Boys and Girls Clubs of America (BGCA), an organization that provides kids around the country with after-school programs. Denzel recalls being just eight years old when he first experienced how important having a positive role model and mentor in your life can be. As a student at the BGCA, he had a mentor who told him that he could do anything that he wanted with his life, and another mentor who would proudly display the college pennants from BGCA alumni to inspire Denzel and his fellow BGCA peers. Now, having achieved his dream of being an actor, Denzel credits the mentors at BGCA as well as mentors and role models from many other areas of his life, with much of his ability to succeed. In fact, he believes in the importance of mentoring so much that he even wrote a book called *A Hand to Guide Me*, which collects stories from more than seventy people across all walks of life about their mentors. Just like Denzel, finding and valuing the mentors and role models in your life will help you achieve your dream!

TYPES OF MENTORS

So, the next obvious question becomes: Where can you look for a mentor who has these qualities and fits with you, your dream, and your journey to reach it? How do you even begin to start looking for such a person? It can definitely seem daunting. Well, the good news is that you actually have a lot of options available to you—you just have to be willing to put some time and effort into looking for them! One of the great things about mentorship in the twenty-first century is that, while your mentor can be someone you are geographically near, they can also be located anywhere around the world. (In my case, one of my mentors was literally *out of this world,* since he was an astronaut spending six months on the International Space Station! But even that distance didn't stop our ability to continue our mentor-mentee relationship.)

The very first step in looking for a mentor is to gain clarity about what you're looking for. This means figuring out what sort of mentorship you want. Are you looking for a formal mentorship with scheduled meetings on a regular basis, or are you looking for a more relaxed relationship? What kind of guidance do you hope to get from your mentor? Do you know what your plans to reach your dream are (think back to the planning you did in chapter 3!) and how a mentor could fit into and help advance those plans?

Generally speaking, there are four main categories or types of mentors that you might encounter: the expert mentor, the champion mentor, the life skills mentor, and the anchor mentor. Not really sure what these titles mean? Don't worry, read on to learn about them!

1. **The expert mentor:** This is someone who has extensive experience and has likely attained great success in the field you're interested in.

"LUCK has NOTHING to DO WITH IT."

2. **The champion mentor:** This is someone who believes in you and your dream and wants to tell the world about you! A champion mentor can help you have the confidence to

believe in yourself and your dream, and can also connect you with others who can help further your progress toward your dream.

"YOU'VE GOT THIS."

"LET US MAKE our DREAMS tomorrow's REALITY."

3. The life skills mentor: This is someone who has demonstrated experience and excellence in life skills, but isn't necessarily in your field of interest.

4. The anchor mentor: This is someone who supports you as you reach for your dream, but who knows you as a person beyond your dream and, above anything else, has your best interests in mind. An anchor mentor might serve as a sounding board to work through struggles, make decisions, or otherwise overcome obstacles in relation to your life and dream.

"ALWAYS STAY TRUE TO YOURSELF."

Which Type of Mentor Is Right for You?

What type of mentor are you looking to find? Answer the questions below to help yourself figure out what you're looking for in terms of guidance and mentorship. Circle a number from 1 to 5 to answer each question, with 1 being not important to you at all, 3 being neutral, and 5 being most important to you. It's perfectly okay and normal to find that you have a need for or interest in having a mentor for multiple parts of your life and dream, so don't worry if you can't choose just one type of mentor.

★ How important is it to you to receive advice about the specifics of the field that your dream is in?

   1 2 3 4 5

★ How important is it to you to have someone to advocate for you and your dream?

   1 2 3 4 5

★ How important is it to you to get help with life skills that are not directly related to your field of interest, but that will help you accomplish your dream in the long run? For example, would you want someone who could guide you on things like time management or cultivating perseverance and commitment?

   1 2 3 4 5

★ How important is it to you to have someone to support *you* unconditionally and help you develop a broad plan to reach your dream?

1 2 3 4 5

Now take a look at how you answered these questions and see which one or ones you ranked the highest (or most important). If it was the first question, you're likely looking for an expert mentor; if it was the second, it seems you're in the market for a champion mentor; the third, a life skills mentor; and the fourth, an anchor mentor!

IDENTIFY A MENTOR

Once you've thought about what type of mentor you're most interested in, you're ready to start actually looking! You might be considering people who are in your life already—or you might want to broaden your search to someone who's not in your life quite yet, but who you could enlist to be your mentor. But remember, you don't have to rush out and find a mentor right away! Mentorships are the most powerful when they're not forced. Take what you're learning from this chapter and allow it to bounce around in your mind until you find the right person and the time feels right to enter into a mentorship with them. (And hey, if that right time is now, that's cool too!) Being patient and keeping an open mind—and open eyes, and open ears—is actually the very first method for finding a mentor.

As you work your way through the world, keep the idea of mentorship in the back of your mind and be on the lookout for people who impress you with their can-do attitude, wisdom, or any other qualities you're looking for in a mentor. Search for people whose ethics and values line up with yours, or who challenge you in a good way, and for people whose experiences you believe you could learn and benefit from. It might even help to think about fictional characters you admire from your favorite books, TV shows, or movies, and to consider what attributes they have that make you admire them! Are those same attributes things you can look for in people in real life?

You might be surprised where and when you meet someone who could end up being a lifelong mentor to you. True story: I met one of my mentors, Astronaut Luca Parmitano, while standing in the security line of an airport! Thinking about mentorship now means that you'll pay attention to the people around you and be aware enough not to miss out on any randomly lucky opportunities that might come your way.

Who Do You Admire?

Let's have some fun! In this activity you're going to make two lists of fictional characters: one list of characters you like and admire, and one of characters you dislike or despise. (For example, my dislike list would include Dolores Umbridge. *Eek!*) For each character, write down their name alongside a couple of their attributes that explain why you to view them either positively or negatively.

Positive Characters

Negative Characters

Where to Find a Mentor

In order to find someone who could potentially make a great mentor for you, you might have to do some research. It's definitely possible that the mentors that you need and deserve are already in your life in some way, and that you just have to get that relationship going. If so, that's great! You're well on your way. But if you've thought about the people in your life and just don't feel like there's anyone who is a good fit to mentor you—don't worry! This definitely does NOT mean that you don't still have access to lots of great potential mentors. Let's dive in and take a look at the various ways to search for a mentor.

The easiest place to start looking for a mentor in is within your own community. Think about who you personally know and admire. Remember, unless you're looking for an expert mentor (someone from within the same field as your dream who will be able to help you with particular or technical advice), your mentor doesn't have to be entirely connected to your dream. Really cast your net out! People you might consider could include family members, teachers, coaches, family friends, your friends' parents, troop leaders, and more. The important thing here is to look for people who display the characteristics that you're looking for in a mentor (just like we talked about earlier in the chapter!).

If you're not having any luck finding someone right within your immediate circles, try expanding your search by looking at nearby communities. There are likely some people there who you're aware of, but don't have personal contact with—at least not yet. Here are just a few suggestions of ways to start looking nearby:

1. **Find a volunteer position** or internship in the field that your dream is in. Not only are volunteer jobs and internships great for the community and great for your résumé, they also expose you to a whole new circle of people! They're fantastic ways to look for a mentor because the people who are in charge of managing interns and volunteers are much more likely than the average person to be familiar with, have experience with, and be open to mentoring someone. I found one of my most important mentors, who has advised me extensively on graduate school and career options, during my time interning at the Space Life Sciences Labs at Kennedy Space Center.

2. **Look for local clubs** or groups in your field of interest. For example, if (like me) you're interested in space, you could look for a stargazing club. If you're interested in art, you could look for an art group, painting class, knitting circle, or any other gatherings of artists in your area. Or if you're interested in creating or inventing, you could look for a maker space or a local fix-it clinic near you. It might not seem immediately obvious, but with a little bit of creativity, you can find a club or group related to any dream you might have. Even if it's not squarely focused on the

exact idea of your dream, you can use it as an opportunity to build skills you'll need down the road! So if your dream includes public speaking or performing of any sort (that might mean anyone who has a dream of being a singer, a musician, an actor, a newscaster, a podcast host, a voice-over artist, a motivational speaker, a teacher, a politician, and the list goes on . . .), you could look for a local Toastmasters club, join your school's debate team, or find a community theater to be a part of. You might not be old enough to officially join some of the groups that you find, but even so, reaching out to the group's leaders and expressing your interest to them forms a bond that exposes you to the members and is likely to impress.

3. **Research the alumni of your school** or any other organization you've been involved in. You never know, one of them might be in the field that your dream is in or otherwise have experiences and qualities that you're interested in. Having the common bond of being alumni gives you a great jumping-off point to reach out to anyone you find and are interested in learning more about.

4. **Do some research online!** The world is so much larger now than it ever has been, because technology allows us to connect with anyone, anywhere. A great first step is to make a list of what qualities, skills, and attributes you are

looking for in a mentor. Try to be as specific as possible! Is it important to you that your mentor has knowledge or connections in the field that your dream is in? Use the list that you've made to do some online research. You can use the internet to look for someone in your field of interest, or with other qualities that are important to you, who you could enter into a digitally based mentorship with. You can also research people in your immediate or nearby communities to find someone who'd be a great mentor for you that you just weren't aware of before! For example, if your dream is to learn how to paint, you could look for painting groups, art classes, art or paint supply stores, galleries, or professional painters who are located near you. You could then reach out digitally, or in the case of having found a paint or art store, make an in-person visit. Always remember, of course, to be safe about anyone you reach out to online, and to always let an adult know what you're doing.

Your Mentor Dream Team!

Make a list of people you admire and would like to emulate. Start big—list people who are your role models, regardless of how realistic it would be to actually have them mentor you (think Barack Obama,

Simone Biles, or Malala Yousafzai). Don't worry about choosing people based on your access to them or their ability to mentor you. This is your dream team of mentors! Think of it like you're assembling your own personal superhero squad to chase after your dream, or like you're putting together your presidential cabinet and the first order of business is to follow your dream. Next to each person on your dream team, write down one word describing what you admire the most about them.

1. _____

2. _____

3. _____

4. _____

5. _____

Now take each of the one-word descriptions you wrote about your dream team above and rewrite them below. Next to each of these attributes, list the names of as many people as you can think of who you think demonstrate that particular trait, and who you would appreciate being mentored by. Think of people you don't already know but could reach out to.

1. _____

2. _____

3. _____

4. _____

5. _____

Finally, make one more list. Once again, write down the five attributes that you admire in your dream team of mentors. This time, next to each attribute, write the name of someone from your life who you actually know and who you think displays this attribute!

1. _____

2. _____

3. _____

4. _____

5. _____

Remember, finding a mentor isn't a race! Don't feel discouraged if you've looked in all of the areas listed above and haven't found a mentor, or mentors, who you're super excited about. While we can certainly raise our chances of finding a great mentor by knowing what we're looking for, keeping an open mind and open eyes, and increasing the range of our communities, there's still a certain amount of chance involved! That's something that just can't be rushed or forced—but don't worry, you'll find your mentor, or mentors, when the time is right.

HOW TO ASK SOMEONE TO MENTOR YOU!

Okay, so you've done all the hard work of sorting out your priorities, deciding what you're looking for, and putting the effort into finding potential mentors—and you've even been lucky enough to find someone you think might be a great fit for you. Amazing! But . . . now what? How do you go from making this mentorship an idea in your mind to an actual, real thing? Well, as with any relationship, a mentorship is a two-way street: they have to want to mentor you as much as you want them to be your mentor. Now's the time to get to know them more and see if they're on board!

Sometimes mentorships develop completely on their own with no need, and no room, for a formal request or declaration. In these instances, you and your mentor may not even be thinking of yourselves as mentor and mentee. If this isn't the case for you, though, it's up to you to get the relationship going, and there is absolutely nothing wrong with flat out asking someone to be your mentor.

Asking someone to be your mentor might seem scary or uncomfortable, and especially so because your mentor-to-be should be someone you admire, but I promise, it's really no big deal. Let's start by thinking about the worst-case scenario that could happen if you were to ask someone to mentor you—and you'll see, it really isn't even all that bad! At the worst, asking someone to be your mentor might result in a brief moment of awkwardness for both you and them if they say no (which they might), but if you think about it, you're no worse off than if you hadn't asked at all.

Having someone decline to mentor you usually isn't personal at all—it most likely has to do with them. You know the

saying "It's not you, it's me"? In this case it's probably true—there are all kinds of reasons for someone to not want to become a mentor. They could be too busy, they might already be mentoring someone else and feel that they're at their personal capacity, or they might even lack the confidence in themselves to believe that they would be able to mentor you well. These are all just potential reasons someone might say no—there are definitely others, depending on the specific situation of the person you're asking. The important thing to remember if someone does decline your mentorship request is that no matter what their reason is (and you may never know what their reason for saying no was), it probably wasn't about you.

In the case that someone does say no, it's important to handle that response with tact and maturity. You can simply thank them for letting you make your request and move right along. I guarantee you that whether they say yes or no, your potential mentor will feel honored and flattered by your asking them to mentor you.

Now that we've realized that someone saying no isn't so scary, let's think about a more positive outcome: they say yes! Woohoo! It's entirely likely that someone will say yes—so many people get excited about the opportunity to help an up-and-comer who's interested in what they do. Remember what we just said about a potential mentor feeling flattered by your request? That can definitely come into play here.

So now that you've had the pep talk to get your confidence

all amped up (yeah, you got this!), and you're on board with the general *idea* of asking someone to be your mentor, I'm sure you're wondering one very specific thing: How, precisely, do you actually *ask* someone to be your mentor? Well, there's no one answer to that; it depends on your particular situation with your potential mentor. But one thing that doesn't change, no matter what, is that, as we previously talked about, you'll need to have done your research on them. Reading up on their history, looking at where they're currently working or what they're currently doing, and going deeper than just a quick Google search will help you figure out how to ask this specific person to be your mentor. The good news is that you've already done all the researching, so now you get to just review it and use it! Yay! The next piece of good news is that there are a few different options of how to ask someone to mentor you that you can choose from.

If the person you have in mind is someone you know, you could call them, send them an email, or ask them in person. If it's someone you don't see very often or you don't personally know, you still have two options: you could send them an email with your request in it (or better yet, send an email asking for a short in-person or video meeting, if possible), or you could cold-call them. Cold-calling is when you call someone without any advance notice.

Whether you know the person

already or not, whether you're emailing, meeting in person, or cold-calling to ask someone to be your mentor, you can use essentially the same script. The good news is that it's a pretty simple one—here's how it goes: If you don't already know the person you're reaching out to, you'll want to introduce yourself with your full name and any information that might connect you to them (this info could be that you're both alumni from a certain summer camp or school, or that you grew up in the same county). Then you can go on to explain that you're reaching out because you're looking for guidance and mentorship. Mention something outstanding they've done in their life or career that inspires you (this is why you want them to be your mentor in the first place!), and then request a short meeting with them at their convenience. If they don't live near you, or if meeting in person is for some reason just not an option, you can also ask for a virtual meeting on FaceTime, Skype, or some other video-chat platform. The whole idea is to just get a conversation going!

Make Your Own Cold-Call Script!

Use the template on the next page to make your own "cold-call" script to request someone to mentor you. Feel free to fill in just the blank spaces, or customize it to be more specific to you! Remember, the goals here are to be professional, respectful, and quick.

Hello, _____, my name is _____. You and I both _____. I'm calling you today because _____. I've been a big fan of yours since _____ and was especially inspired by your _____ in _____. I was wondering whether you might have any time in the next couple of weeks to meet with me and offer some advice and guidance. Please let me know, at your convenience.

Yours truly,

_____

(Obviously only use that sign-off for an email, and not if you're actually speaking on the phone or video chatting with someone!)

Once you've made contact with your po-tential mentor, it's time to follow through on the meeting! Make sure that you show your interest in and respect for the time that your potential mentor is sharing with you by showing up pre-

pared. You've already done your research about them—now all you really have to do to be ready is to know what you're looking for from the mentorship and to have some questions that you'd like them to answer. These questions could include specifics about the field they're in (such as something they recently did that you found interesting or exciting) and about their previous experience with mentorship (it would be totally fair game to ask direct questions like, *Have you ever mentored someone in the past? And if so, how did it go?* or *Are you currently mentoring anyone?*). They should definitely include questions about what mentoring you might look like (how much time they're able to spend, how they like to communicate, what they could help you with, and what they might expect from you). It's perfectly okay to write any of this down on a notepad and bring it in to the meeting with you—whatever makes you feel comfortable (plus it shows your potential mentor that you cared enough to prepare!).

Conduct a Practice Interview!

Conduct a mock interview with a trusted person in your life (someone like your mom, dad, teacher, or coach). Do what you can to make it feel like the real deal so that you can get the best practice possible. This might include wearing the same type of clothing you would to talk to the person you think you want to be your mentor or trying to pretend you don't know the person you're talking to yet (in the latter case you get to practice introducing yourself and explaining why you've reached out to them). Ask them the questions that you're planning to ask in your real interview, or think of some other, similar types of questions that you might be able to ask your practice person to get a conversation going with them. Afterward, ask them to tell you what they thought you did well and what they think you could improve on for your real interview. Write these comments down below so that you can reflect on them before your real interview!

BE A MENTOR—AT EVERY STAGE AND EVERY AGE!

Here's one of the most exciting things about mentorship, though—and one of the least well known: just like how we can all benefit from having a mentor, we also all have the ability to be mentors! You might be thinking: *Yeah, someday after I've grown up, reached my dream, gained more experience, sure, then I could mentor somebody else.* And while that is true, and I totally believe that you'll make a great mentor someday in the future, I want you to know that you can actually be a great mentor right here and now, as you currently are.

That's right: you don't have to wait until you're classically successful, any certain age, or really anything else to be a mentor. Think about all the reasons that someone may agree (or might have already agreed) to mentor you—do any of those also apply to you? Becoming a mentor is a way to give back to your community, to pass on the same help you've received to someone else, to feel a sense of accomplishment and pride about doing something good, and even for you to personally learn and grow—and those are things you can do at any age or stage of life! Read on to learn everything you need to know about why you should not only have a mentor, but why you should think about becoming one yourself!

Without a doubt, I've been able to become a role model and help others find their dreams (including by writing this book that you're reading right now!) because of an early mentor of mine. When I was sixteen years old, I worked with Astronaut Luca Parmitano of the European Space Agency during his six months on the International Space Station. We created a brand-new role for me: Earth Liaison. The goal of this partnership was for me to use my large social media presence to share Luca's experiences living and working in space with more people here on Earth—and specifically, to reach audiences that might respond better to me than to Luca, like young people, and especially girls.

During Luca's time in space, I truly started to recognize what he had clearly already seen: that I could be a role model and a leader. As his Earth Liaison, I hosted Q and A's between him and my social media followers, wrote and published weekly briefings of his activities on the Space Station, and created campaigns such as #CatchLuca, where I challenged people to go out at night and take a picture of the ISS orbiting overhead and then send it to me or post it online. I also visited countless schools and classrooms, in person or through video calls, to talk to students about life on board the ISS. I was astonished at the incredibly positive reactions that I got during these school visits. I realized that the reason the students I spoke to reacted so strongly and enthusiastically was because I was like them.

Because I wasn't an astronaut yet—or even an adult—I was able to connect more with the kids I was visiting and talking with. I was acting as an intermediary role model: someone who was working toward getting to space, but was close enough to the kids I was visiting that they could look at me and say, *Hey, I think I could follow that same path too someday!* rather than feeling intimidated or confused by someone who was so many steps ahead in life. I learned firsthand how important it is to have role models who haven't yet achieved their dreams and goals—and because of that, I know that you can fill that same role.

Sometimes being a role model means showing the messy middle, the intermediary steps that you took (or are taking) on your path toward your dream. That helps others who are just starting out to realize that reaching their dreams might not be easy, seamless, or quick. This idea is especially important when it comes to girls and women, because we have a tendency to judge ourselves more critically and hold ourselves to higher standards than boys and men do. We tend to see ourselves as not qualified enough or not ready for something, when in reality, we are. Having a role model who talks about or shows that the path to success is often windy and unpredictable, and includes mistakes and failures, can make all the difference in a girl or woman's ability to believe in herself and her own path to success.

You don't have to—and in many instances you shouldn't necessarily—wait until you're a recognized leader or figure of success to act as a role model. You can still be a role model even if you don't yet consider yourself to be a leader or a success yet! You are never too young, too old, too inexperienced, too unsuccessful, too new, or too anything to be a role model and mentor to someone else.

Each and every one of us has the capability to make the same kind of impact on others that mentors can have (or may have already had) on us. Showing support to others and lending a hand when you're able to can make huge ripples. By supporting each other and raising one another up, we can help dreamers reach for their dreams right now and for future generations, and you have a part to play! We all need help to reach our dreams, and a mentor (or more likely, multiple mentors!) may just be the person you've been looking for who can help you achieve your dream. Whether you're the one being mentored or mentoring, why not give mentorship a shot?

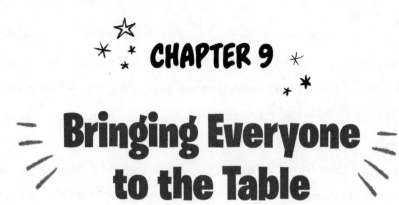

CHAPTER 9

Bringing Everyone to the Table

If there isn't a seat at the table for me, I'm making my own table.

—Nabela Noor, digital content creator

I f there's one thing that I hope has come across so far in this book, it is that you are truly not alone in your process of dreaming big and achieving your dreams. You are part of a community—a community that starts with your close circle of family, friends, confidants, mentors, and other supporters, and then ranges all the way out to include the entirety of humanity. These communities can be incredibly helpful—and often even necessary—in achieving your dreams and goals. Nobody achieves anything alone—we all need others.

But being part of a community doesn't only mean that you

get support, belief, and help from others—it also gives you an obligation to contribute back! In some of this book's earlier chapters, we explored some of the ways that we, as dreamers and doers, can give back and contribute positively to our communities—we've talked about things like being disruptors (remember that from chapter 4?) and being role models and mentors to others (just a few pages back in chapter 8!). In this chapter, we'll take a look at another important way that we can both benefit from and contribute to our communities: by being aware of our differences, and actively working to bring others (especially those who are different from us) to the table along with us.

This is something that each and every one of us can do, regardless of where we are in the process of achieving our dreams, what our specific dreams are, or any other unique individual factor. This chapter will talk about both why and how you (yes, you!) can bring everyone to the table so that you can get right to being your awesome self, chasing your dream, and giving back to your community.

WHAT IS THE TABLE?

But wait—what's this "table" I've just mentioned? And what does it actually mean to "have a seat at the table" or to "bring others to the table"? You may—or may not—have heard these phrases thrown around before, but even if you have, they might still be a bit confusing. So let's talk about what they actually mean!

The first thing to know is that when people use these phrases, they usually aren't talking about a literal table, but rather about a metaphorical table where you and other decision makers and leaders gather to set the future in motion. At its core, saying that someone has a seat or a spot at the table means that that person (you!) has credibility, influence, and decision-making abilities. It implies that you have the power to have your voice be heard and respected—and that can mean your actual, literal voice, or it can mean that your opinions and ideas get taken into consideration. Your seat at the table gives you an active role in effecting change, accomplishing things, and setting the agenda for what comes next.

Since having a seat at the table is all about getting a say in what happens, it seems pretty obvious that you'd want that for

your own dream and future. In fact, everything we've been talk-ing about up until now in this book should help give you ways to do just that! So, why then are we focusing in on this idea for a whole new chapter? Well, for two main reasons: First, because it's incredibly helpful for your dream, and your ability to achieve that dream, to have other people at your table offering up a range of different opinions and ideas. And second, because it's also a great thing to sit at the tables of other people's dreams, or even to help create those tables in the first place, so that those around you can reach for their own dreams as well!

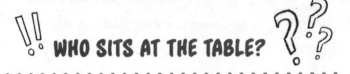

WHO SITS AT THE TABLE?

Now you know what this magical table is, and what it means to have a seat at it. But at this point you're probably wonder-ing: *Who all gets to sit at the table, how do they get that seat, and why?* The answer to these questions, of course, depends on whose table you're talking about—so to keep it simple, let's look at who gets a seat at *your* table. As we just saw, this table is a metaphor for the group of people who have the power to make and implement decisions. Given that, the very first seat at your table should go to . . . you! One of the beautiful things about following your dream is that you don't have to ask any-one else for a seat—instead, you get to make your own table and sit at the head of it! This means that you steer the ship, make the final decisions, and choose who else sits with you.

So far you're the only one sitting at the table you've made, but I'm sure you'll agree with me that you want to fill your table up with people who will help you reach your dream. These people might include the mentors and role models from chapter 8; your parents or other family members; your teachers, coaches, advocates, peers, and many more—it's completely up to you who you invite and involve in advising and guiding you on your path to your dream.

There are lots of options out there, clearly, but here's one key idea to keep in mind: every single person you share your table with should be someone who will lift you up. And here's another super important thing to consider: as you're filling out the seats at your table, one of the most crucial things to do is to create space for people who are different from you, and then value the unique perspective and abilities that these differences give us all. Truly, making space for other people who come from different backgrounds, possess different abilities and resources, and have had different experiences makes us smarter, more capable, and all around better—and in turn is incredibly helpful for you and your ability to reach your dream!

CREATING A DIVERSE TABLE

Let's talk for a minute about what having different people at your table means, and what diversity can look like. Diversity, at its core, is merely the state of being made up of different components. Which is really cool because, when you think about it, there's nothing more human than being different. Truly, no single human is a carbon copy of another. All the way down to the very smallest molecules that make us up, we are all unique individuals. This is even true of identical twins—despite looking identical and having started out as the same zygote (a fertilized egg cell), identical twins do not actually have completely identical DNA! And it's not just our physical components that make us different and unique—we all have different histories and life experiences, different cultures we grew up in or currently exist in, different ways of thinking, different skills and capabilities, and so much more. These are the things that make us who we are—and who we each are is completely different from anyone else.

We're all different, and as such, we're all a part of the diversity of humanity. Need further convincing that each and every one of us adds to our communal or even global diversity? Take a look at this list of just some of the areas that diversity includes, and ask yourself if you see differences between yourself and anyone else you know in one (or more) of these categories: race, gender, sexual orientation, language/language abilities, education, physical ability, neurological ability, religion, age, nationality, socioeconomic status, and culture.

All of these dissimilarities among us result in different viewpoints, different ways of thinking, different ways of approaching problems and coming up with solutions, access to and retention of different kinds of knowledge and resources, and more. Because of that, as we gather at our metaphorical tables, we each bring something different with us—and any one background, set of life experiences, or skill set alone will not be as helpful and powerful as a collection of them combined together could be. We are all better when we recognize, respect, and value the ways that people who are different from us can positively enhance our own skills, abilities, opinions, and more. And we are better off when we invite and welcome a diverse range of voices to the table.

Imagine, for instance, that your dream is to start your own company—maybe a home bakery. As you're trying to make that happen, think: Who would you want to sit at your table for this endeavor? How successful do you think your bakery business would be if the only people you involved in it were friends of yours who all loved baking desserts just like you do? I'm sure your cupcakes, macarons, and anything else you created would all be to-die-for delicious, but that wouldn't matter if you had a hard time spreading the word about your business, budgeting your expenses, or doing lots of other non-baking-related things that would all be necessary for your dream to be a success. Now imagine if, instead, you had a table filled with people representing diverse backgrounds and viewpoints—the possibilities for your bakery open up way wider!

Maybe a friend of yours is from Turkey and has an

incredible recipe for making baklava that you can add to your menu. Maybe another person you know is a really great artist, or a great writer, and can help come up with ads and flyers to spread the word about the bakery. Maybe someone else in your community doesn't know a whole lot about baking but has a mind for numbers or organization and can help manage the business. The possibilities are endless! The more diverse experiences, skill sets, and opinions you bring to the table, the better off you'll be. And this doesn't just hold true for big, involved, or complex dreams (like starting a business). I guarantee you that, in some way or another, your dream, no matter how big, small, or in-between it is, is just like that hypothetical home bakery business—you will be more successful at chasing after and accomplishing it if you ensure that your table has a wide diversity of people with different skills, life experiences, interests, and abilities.

Here's one out-there way of thinking about all of this: an intriguing result of having had humans living in space for the past couple of decades is that we've learned that what we might think of as "everyday" things are not actually so commonplace when you're living in space. Some of the things that we take for granted, that we probably do subconsciously and never even give a second thought to, are completely different—and often much more difficult—for someone in space. For example, did you know that the types of socks that astronauts wear are different from those we wear here on Earth? Astronauts in space live in microgravity—basically, they're floating all the time! This means that if they want to stay in one place (to eat, to type on a computer, or to do any other type of work) they need to be strapped in or holding on to something to avoid floating away. But astronauts can't always give up a hand to hold themselves in place—can you imagine how difficult it would be to do everything one-handed? Instead, they use their feet to hook onto railings, doorways, or anything else they can reach to help hold themselves in place.

But while using their feet to stay put is a great solution to the problem of constantly floating away in microgravity, it also comes with drawbacks. It can cause pain and even damage after a while, and astronauts can actually end up with calluses on the tops of their feet instead of the bottoms! Pretty wild, right? To counter this, astronauts have special socks that they can wear to help redistribute some of the pressure across their feet to avoid overusing any one spot.

The reason I'm telling you this weird story about space feet isn't just because I think it's really cool and interesting (though it totally is), but because I think that it highlights how differently two people can experience what might seem at first glance like the same event or action—and how those differing experiences can be based on specific circumstances or environments. Putting on socks is probably one of the things that many of us do every day without even thinking about it. We take our socks for granted because we've never had to think or worry about how important they might be. If you're out of fresh socks, or can't find any, or for any other reason decide not to put on your socks on any given day, it's generally no big deal. But this isn't true for astronauts in space—space socks are absolutely vital to their comfort and long-term health! Our experiences living on Earth are completely different from the experiences of people living in space.

But while the comparison between living on Earth and living in space makes it relatively easy to see just how different people can experience the same basic thing in wildly different manners, this phenomenon is definitely not reserved just for drastic differences in living locations—it occurs in every single part of our lives. Just like how you might not have realized how important socks can be to one particular group of people, other people might not even know to think about particular things that concern you or become a factor in your everyday life. There are people who might struggle with things that you've never thought to struggle with, or that are easy, accessible, or second nature to you but may not be to everyone else.

And this all comes back to creating a diverse table for yourself and for others. The idea of bringing everyone to the table is centered around understanding that each of us is a unique individual and that we all have different histories, different perspectives, and different experiences in the world. It means being open to thinking about and learning about these differences, and then using that knowledge both to help our own dreams grow in a way that takes others' ideas into account, and to do what we can to alleviate some of the struggles or barriers that

we don't personally face but that others do. Bringing everyone to the table means trying to bridge the gaps we face in order to give each and every one of us equal footing and an equal shot at achieving our dreams.

Recognize Diversity in Your Life! ✏

Think of someone in your life who is different from you—maybe they are a different race, have a different religion, or live in a different environment, or maybe they just have a different set of skills, passions, and interests. Write down the ways that they have improved or impacted your life—big or small—and how the thing that makes them different from you brought something new to the table that you would not have been able to bring on your own, with your own unique experiences and passions.

_____

_____

_____

_____

_____

_____

_____

_____

HOW TO BRING EVERYONE TO THE TABLE!

We've established what the table is, who gets to sit at it, and why different voices are important to include. So now the big question becomes: How can *I* implement this? As with many of the other skills we've talked about in this book, the thought might seem daunting—but luckily, there are lots of different ways to go about doing this! Let's dive in and take a look at few ideas here, and then you can pick the one (or more!) that sounds like the best fit for your own life and dream.

USE YOUR VOICE!

Having a seat at the table (whether your own or someone else's) means that you are in a position to have your voice be heard. This is an exciting opportunity, and not one that everyone gets, so it's up to you to advocate both for yourself and for those who might otherwise feel voiceless. Speaking up for those who may not yet have found their voice can help to bring others to the table, because it gives them the space to find their bearings at whatever table they're joining. Don't waste the opportunity to use your voice to make change for yourself and others in your community!

You can do this in a number of ways, but there's one that I've found to be extremely effective and also pretty simple: ask

questions, frequently. Some questions might feel silly to ask, or seem daunting for some particular reason, but I promise you that there is basically no question not worth asking. And in addition to the questions having value to you personally, asking questions helps the people around you too! Here's something to think about: that question that you were hemming and hawing over, trying to decide whether it was important or worthwhile enough to ask? I guarantee that you're not the only one who had that question, or the only one who learned from the answer. Think about it this way—can you remember a time in your life when you had a question that you were wondering about but weren't confident enough to ask, but then someone else asked that same question and you felt grateful to hear the answer? Well, that happens more often than you might think, to many people and for many reasons. All of which is to say, when you use your voice to ask questions, everyone benefits!

Asking questions isn't the only way to use your voice (not by far!). One other method that I'd like to highlight here, because it's just so important, is: voice your opinions. Your thoughts and opinions matter! Truly, they do—you absolutely have a right to your own unique and individual ideas, preferences, suggestions, and more. And while this is always true, it's even more important in regard to your own dream. When you speak up, you contribute your own element into the diverse mix of the table that you're sitting at, which benefits everyone sitting around it, and can have an impact on your own dream or on someone else's. Sharing your thoughts and opinions with others (which is to say, voicing your opinions!) will both positively help you and help to bring others to the table!

Nabela Noor is an international sensation as a beauty blogger, digital content creator, and activist for inclusivity, diversity, and equality. She has millions of followers on social media, has worked with major beauty brands, and even founded a nonprofit to provide housing, education, and other necessary resources to people living in poverty in her family's home country, Bangladesh. Looking at her now (and seeing her success), it's hard to imagine that there was ever a time when Nabela felt like she didn't have a seat at the table—but that's actually the reason she started off on social media in the first place, and used it to build the base of her platform! Growing up, Nabela had a passion for beauty and fashion, but she felt that society's standards for beauty were too narrow and didn't include her, even though she knew she was beautiful. A big part of this was that she didn't see a whole lot of people who looked like her represented in traditional media. As a first-generation South Asian immigrant in the US and a plus-size woman, Nabela decided that if she wanted to see media and content that truly fit, resonated, and represented her and others like her, she would just have to make that content herself. And that's exactly what she did! Rather than allow anyone or anything else to dictate where she belonged, Nabela created her own table to make sure that her unique voice was heard and valued. Not only that, Nabela ensured that her table was filled with a diverse and inclusive group of people so that others wouldn't have to struggle to find representation and belonging the way she had—and she's been crushing it ever since! Just like Nabela, you can use your voice and your own unique and individual skills and abilities to create a table that fits you—and others.

CELEBRATE YOUR DIFFERENCES!

Another way that you can help to bring more people to the table, no matter whose table it is, is by showing appreciation for the people around you who are different from you. While it may seem like the best course of action is always to find what we have in common and look past the things that make us different, that couldn't be further from the truth! Research has shown that ignoring our differences in an effort to not discriminate based on those differences actually has the opposite effect—instead, doing so can decrease the opportunities available and accessible and even cause unique and special voices and experiences to be hidden or lost! Instead, try to actively think about both your similarities with people *and* your differences! Looking at the differences in the people around us can be a great way to learn more about other people's lives, experiences, and dreams, and can help you both make space available at the table for lots of people and also value your own uniqueness!

Celebrate Your Differences by Comparing and Contrasting

Make a list of your particular skills, talents, and abilities, and then make another list of all your resources. Then think about the people in your life and pick someone who is different from you in some way (maybe a friend, classmate, or someone else!). Ask this person to make the same lists that you made, and then compare your list with theirs. Is there anything that really surprises you? Are there things on the other person's list that you hadn't anticipated? How do the lists make you feel? Are there things that the other person brings to the table that you're thankful for? Think about how your dream would be affected by the differences you notice in this person!

_____   _____

_____   _____

_____   _____

_____   _____

_____   _____

_____   _____

_____   _____

_____   _____

_____   _____

SHARE YOUR SKILLS!

My favorite way of bringing other people to the table? That would be teaching them skills that I have that they might find useful as well—and asking them to do the same for me! I like to call this skill swapping. It can be especially helpful if you're sharing a skill that seems easy or second nature to you but could feel difficult or inaccessible to someone else, or the other way around, and it's even better if you can share skills that help forward each of your dreams. One of the really exciting things about sharing your skills with other people is that doing so can take a variety of forms. Sometimes skill swapping might be a straight trade—you teach someone else how to do something, and in exchange, they teach you something else. Other times it

might be more of a skill share than a swap—an opportunity for you to give someone something (such as a skill, ability, or resource that you have and want to share)

without the expectation of anything in return! And likewise, you may at some point find yourself the beneficiary of a one-sided skill share.

Of course, the way you go about swapping or sharing your skills and abilities with others will depend on your (and their) unique circumstances, as well as what type of swap you're engaging in, but there are a few general tips that apply to many instances.

✓ *Decide why you want to share your skills with someone. Is it because you're looking for something and want to trade? Is it because you want to help someone else by sharing your unique skills? Is it because someone else has asked you to teach or share something with them? Knowing your motives will help guide the rest of your skill-sharing experience.*

✓ *Determine what skills you have that you could share with somebody else. You can start to figure this out by asking some basic questions, like:* What am I good at? Does someone else need or want this? Is there a way I can increase access to my table—or join someone else's table—by sharing this skill?

✓ *Be brave! Skill swapping might require you to step outside your comfort zone, whether by learning a new skill, asking for help, or offering help to someone else. It's perfectly okay and normal to feel a little bit uncomfortable in these instances, but knowing that what you're doing will broaden your and others' tables will hopefully give you the courage to face that discomfort and engage anyway!*

Step Out of Your Comfort Zone

Are you a STEM lover, maybe someone who is comfortable doing science projects or math equations? Do you have a friend who likes entirely different things, one who might rather play the piano or write a story? Or is it the opposite, and you're the creative writer with a friend who loves trying out new experiments and projects? Think about the things you love, the components of you that make you strive for your dream, and then challenge yourself to find someone with different interests or hobbies. Step out of your comfort zone by joining them in one of their favorite activities! Put down your telescope (or whatever it is that you spend a lot of your time using) and go make up a dance with your friend who is a dancer. Then turn the tables! When you're done, invite your friend to put aside their dancing shoes and help you with a science experiment. Take note of the ways you can help each other, even in doing things that aren't your usual passions, and write them below.

_____

_____

_____

_____

_____

♡♡ KINDNESS MATTERS ⌒⌒⌒

Kindness makes the world go round. Well, not literally of course (the world goes round because of conserved rotational energy from the protoplanetary disk that our solar system was formed out of), but figuratively, kindness is what it's all about. What I've learned, and what you've probably experienced in life as well, is that relationships are built and maintained through kindness and reciprocity. Essentially what this means is that a relationship—such as your relationship with your community—can't be a one-way street. You have to be willing to act with kindness and compassion toward others if you hope to receive the same. If you want your community to support your dream, believe in you, and help you reach your dream, then you have to do the same for others.

You can think of your relationship with your community like a "take a penny, leave a penny" dish. It's okay and expected and normal to take a penny (or in this case, to take support, help, etc.) from the dish (or in this case, from your community). That's the whole point of the "take a penny, leave a penny" dish existing! But what happens if people only take from the dish, even in moderation, and nobody ever actually leaves a penny in the dish? Pretty soon the dish will be empty, and the next person who needs a penny won't be able to take one (and that next person might even be you!). This same idea holds true for the resources of our communities, such as help, support, connections, opportunities, materials, and more. Our communities support us—

but if we want to see them be able to continue to support us in reaching for our dreams, and for them to also be able to support others in reaching for their dreams in the future, it's important that we not only take from the community, but also give back to it.

Giving back to your community isn't just important as a means of helping others. In fact, doing good is just plain good for you! Doing good things—such as supporting someone and helping them to achieve their dream, believing in them, or helping to make space at the table for them—feels good. Being generous, kind, and helpful has been shown to decrease stress, produce endorphins (which are basically happy chemicals in your brain), promote good mental health, and cause a sense of satisfaction and accomplishment. The Longevity Project, which is the most comprehensive study on living a long life ever conducted, even found that helping others was the single most important factor within human control that could help increase life expectancy!

Put plainly: decades of research have shown that doing good is good for us. And paying it forward—which is when you do something good for someone else without the expectation of receiving anything in return—now or in the future, is a huge part of that! Paying it forward means doing something good because it feels good, and because you remember how you (and your dream!) have been positively impacted by the actions of others, and now you want to make that same positive impact on someone else and their dream.

Doing Good Begets Good

Another thing about doing good deeds is that the simple act of reflecting on times when you've done something good for someone else in the past can make you feel good and want to do more good things in the future! Think back on a time when you did something to help someone else and then write it down in the space below. How do you think that your good deed made the person you were helping feel? How did you feel when you helped them, and how do you feel now when you think about it? Based on your answers to these questions, do you think that you would want to try to help someone again in the future?

At the end of the day, dreams (no matter how big or small, and no matter how long they take to accomplish) require a lot of work—and it takes a community of people, with their diverse backgrounds and unique skills, access to resources, and ways of thinking to help make a dream come true. Bringing others to the table can help you in so many ways, both in terms of reaching for your dream and in helping you feel good about yourself, and it's also an incredibly powerful thing to support and encourage others to follow their dreams and to have agency and power over their own lives and paths. Now it's up to you to use your voice, share your skills, and celebrate everyone's uniqueness—and in doing so, you can bring everyone to the table and share in the successes of your dreams together!

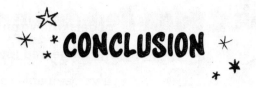

CONCLUSION

_____

_____

_____

_____

TURN TO PAGE 293 TO SEE WHAT TO DO WITH THESE LINES!

Wow! What a journey we've been on together. If you can remember way back to the very first page of this book, when you and I were just starting out exploring your passions, forming them into a dream, and finding your path to reach that dream, I told you that I believed in you, just because you'd picked up this book! Choosing to read this book told me that you were interested in, or even just curious about, discovering your dream and chasing after it. Now that we're here at the end, I hope that, on top of knowing that I believe in you, you know something even more important—that *you* believe in yourself.

Throughout this book, I've shared skills you can use, stories from my own life, examples of role models who've put in the work, activities to get you going, and more, all geared toward helping you, well, *dream big.* I hope that you've been able to learn something new and useful while reading *Dream Big!*, something that's given you confidence in your ability to set out and accomplish your dream, whatever it may be.

You now have a mental tool kit of knowledge, skills, and resources to help you on your path to success. Let's think back on what exactly this tool kit holds:

☑ *You've learned what passion is and how identify what you're passionate about, and then take the next step by shaping that passion into a solid dream.*

☑ *You've learned how to find and take pride in your dream, as well as how to share that dream with others.*

☑ *You've broken your dream down into manageable steps and created a plan to reach each step and, in the end, accomplish your dream as a whole.*

☑ *You've discovered what it means to be disruptive—and how you and your drive to reach your dream will have a ripple effect on many other people.*

☑ *You've faced fears head-on, chosen to take control of those fears before they can control you, and gained skills to manage them.*

☑ *You've learned that failure is inevitable, and that it is actually your friend, not your enemy, in your quest to achieve your dream.*

☑ You've explored how balance can help you to achieve your dreams without losing sight of the rest of the wonderful things around you, and skills for how to strive toward a balance that fits you uniquely.

☑ You've discovered the importance of role models and mentors and learned the different ways that a mentor can affect your path toward your dream, and you've also found out how to cultivate a mentorship. And you've even learned how to be a role model and mentor to others!

☑ And finally, you've learned what it means to have a seat at the table, how important it is to encourage and nurture diversity, and how you can both gain from and give back to your community by bringing others to the table along with you.

Now that you have these skills and tools, it's your time to go out and make your dreams a reality. There's nothing holding you back—now is your time to take action! As you do so, remember that you can always come back to this book to reread any chapters or sections that you find useful, to do the activities included again as many times as you want, to revisit the stories, quotes, or portions that gave you inspiration or motivation, and to generally refresh your mental tool kit for chasing after your dream. It may take some time, and it's entirely possible that you might fall down, stumble, or even lose sight of your path along the way, but in the end I have no doubt that you're going to reach your dream, and possibly even change the world as you go. Now get out there and dream big! I can't wait to see what happens when you do.

Now It's Your Turn!

As you've read through this book, I'm sure you've noticed that each chapter starts with a quote from an inspiring person whose life and work have demonstrated the ideas showcased in that particular chapter. Now that we're here, at the end, you have all the skills and information you need to go out and chase after your dream. This means that it's time for you to be the inspiring person! That's right:

it's your turn to add your awesome words to the collection, because you're just as amazing and inspiring as anyone referenced on the pages you've just read. You can use something you've said in the past, or even make up a quote that current or future you might say! Is there something that you feel truly captures your spirit, your drive, or your passions? Is there a lesson you've learned in life that you think has been super helpful? Is there something you like to say to yourself to keep pushing forward toward your dream? Write it down here!

_____

_____

_____

_____

_____

_____

_____

_____

_____

_____

_____

_____

ACKNOWLEDGMENTS

Writing this book was a joy, a learning experience, and an honor. One of the most amazing parts of writing *Dream Big!* was realizing how many incredible people I have been fortunate enough to have known, worked with, and learned from up to this point in my life. I am so thankful to be able to share the mentorship, advice, lessons, and so much more that I have received.

I'd like to start off by thanking my mom, manager, and nonprofit cofounder, Nicole, for her unending support and belief in my dreams. Additionally, thank you, Mom, for being a role model who taught me the importance of not just talking the talk but following up by walking the walk as well. You have shown me, through your constant example, how to be a force for change and good. Finally, thank you for both being a second set of eyes for my writing and supporting my efforts at every step of writing this book. I love you to Mars and back!

Next, I want to thank all of the amazing people who have helped me produce, create, and publish this book. Thank you to Heather Flaherty, my agent, who originally approached me with the idea of writing a book, for believing in me, helping me develop sample chapters and proposals for *Dream Big!*, and for getting it into the hands of Penguin Random House! Thank you to Talia Benamy, my editor, for helping me to turn the many ideas floating in my head into an actual book! Thank you for being such an incredible source of knowledge, organization, and most importantly, kindness. Thank you to Sarah Coleman for bringing *Dream Big!* to life through artwork that is body positive, diverse, and truly shows the beauty of humans dreaming big. Thank you, Monique Sterling, for finalizing the layout of the text and artwork to make the book look amazing. And finally, I want to thank the entire team at Philomel and Penguin Random House for your work on bringing *Dream Big!* to bookstores and bookshelves.

Additionally, I want to thank the role models, mentors, teachers, and community members who taught me many of the lessons that allowed me to write this book. Thank you to my role models and mentors astronauts Luca Parmitano and Captain Wendy Lawrence; to my wonderful fifth-grade science teacher Mary Hill and my middle school GEMS (Girls in

Engineering Math and Science) coach Dr. Dave Blackburn for sparking a never-ending love of science in me; to my professors at Wellesley College (Dr. Heather Mattila, Dr. Jeff Hughes, Dr. John Cameron, Jocelyne Dolce, and my major advisor, Dr. Dave Ellerby) for your time, care, and expertise in teaching me both academic subjects and life lessons; and to my mentor, boss, and primary investigator Dr. Andrew Schuerger for inviting me to be a part of your Mars-focused lab and research at Kennedy Space Center and for teaching me the skills I will need to be successful in my future career in science. Finally I would like to thank every educator that I have had the pleasure to know, from kindergarten to graduate school, for your work inspiring me. It would take pages to recognize all of the educators who have shaped me over the years.

I would also like to thank all those who have made my nonprofit The Mars Generation, a reality. Thank you to our founding members for believing in our cause right from the start; to all of our current and ongoing members for their support; to all those who have donated their time, money, skills, and talents to make the world a better place through our work. A special thank-you to my board of directors and board of advisors for your time and energy over the years. And a special thank-you to my production team at TMG—your constant work to bring our message to the world is truly out of this world. And a big thank-you to Brian Melendez and the entire legal team of Dykema for all your work in helping with the legal work of building and maintaining a nonprofit.

I'd like to recognize and thank two good friends who have made an impact in my life and in this book. Nancy and Roger McCabe—your nonstop belief in me and support of The Mars Generation and our work has given me so much power and strength to persevere, believe in myself, and also continue my mission with TMG. Thank you!

And finally, I owe my greatest thanks to my family, which consists of amazing women, each of whom has a unique and undeniable strength. Thank you to my sisters, aunts, cousins, and grandmas. Your support of my dreams and endeavors, and the years of your own life experiences which you have shared with me, has truly impacted my path. A special thank-you to my oldest sister and best friend Maddie, for your undying love and support, for always pushing me to be a better, kinder, and more considerate person, and for being president of the "Get Abby off This Planet" club!